Christianity That Counts

Christianity That Counts

Being a Christian in a Non-Christian World

Douglas Groothuis

Baker Books

A Division of Baker Book House Co
Grand Rapids, Michigan 49516

This book is dedicated to the modern evangelical movement: born in greatness, sustained through adversity, and now in jeopardy. May God revive us again to speak the truth in love with transcendent power to a troubled world.

©1994 by Douglas Groothuis

Published by Baker Books
a division of Baker Book House Company
P.O. Box 6287, Grand Rapids, MI 49516-6287

Printed in the United States of America

Library of Congress Cataloging-in-Publication Data

Groothuis, Douglas R., 1957–
    Christianity that counts : being a Christian in a non-Christian world /
Douglas Groothuis.
        p.   cm.
    Includes bibliographical references and index.
    ISBN 0-8010-3868-5
    1. Church and the world. 2. Apologetics—20th century. 3. Witness bearing
(Christianity) I. Title.
BR115.W6G76   1994
261'.1—dc20   94-16000

Chapter 1 first appeared in *CSSH Quarterly* 7 (winter 1984): 13–17; 2, in *Counsel of Chalcedon* (November 1994): 15–17; 3, in *Biblical Worldview* 4 (November 1988): 6–8; 5, in *CSSH Quarterly* 10 (fall 1987): 9–18, 31; 6, in *Critique* 5 (1993): 2–6; 7, in *Christian Research Journal* (spring 1992): 7; 8, in *Critique* 6 (1990): 7–8; 9, in *Reformed Journal* (February 1994); 11, in *CSSH Quarterly* 14 (winter 1991): 13–16; 12, in *Christian Research Journal* (summer 1991): 7; 13, in *Eternity* (May 1985): 32–34; 14, in *Pretty Good News* 6, 1: 7; 17, in *Eternity* (May 1987): 13; 18, in *Critique* 9 (1990): 1–4; 19, in *Christian History* 9, 2 (1990): 39–40; 20, in *Genesis* 3 (1990): 1, 3, 9; 21, in *Christianity Today,* 29 April 1991, 20–23; 22, in *Berea Monograph* 1 (1990); 23, in *SCP Journal* 17, 3 (1992): 24–32; 25, in *Colorado Christian News* (December 1993); 26, in *Crimson Reality* (fall 1993): 11, 18. All are reprinted by permission.

Contents

Introduction

Social critic Theodore Roszak pronounced American Christianity to be "privately engaging, but socially irrelevant." To our shame, this assessment is frequently too true. Outside of subjective experience, Christianity often does not count for as much as it should. Christians may be enthralled with the personal benefits of salvation—or, worse, with the superficial religious entertainments of the evangelical subculture—while neglecting the bracing intellectual and cultural duties enjoined of the followers of Christ in a post-Christian and increasingly anti-Christian world.

Christianity truly is "privately engaging," because the grace of God wrought through Christ Jesus cannot but move the heart of its recipients to joy, wonder, love, and praise. However, Scripture declares that those who are forgiven of their sin and granted eternal life through Christ's finished work ought to be transformed through the renewing of their minds, in order to fathom and implement the will of God "as far as the curse is found" (Rom. 12:1–2; 1 Cor. 10:31). The gospel should invigorate us subjectively, but it should also impel us to demonstrate publicly the reality of Christ: to love God with all our being; to be salt and light; to fight the good fight of faith against the world, the flesh, and the devil; and to take up the cross in service of the one who bore it on our behalf to reconcile us to a holy God. True Christianity is a Christianity that counts in all human experience. Simply put, Christ is bigger than our souls.

After affirming the nature of our salvation, that Christ has "rescued us from the dominion of darkness and brought us into the kingdom of the Son he loves, in whom we have redemption, the forgiveness of sins," Paul majestically proclaims the extent of Christ's lordship:

> He is the image of the invisible God, the firstborn over all creation. For by him all things were created: things in heaven and on earth, visible and invisible, whether thrones or powers or rulers or authorities; all things were created by him and for him. He is before all things, and by him all things hold together. And he is the head of the body, the church; he is the beginning and the firstborn from among the dead, so that in everything he might have the supremacy. [Col. 1:15–18]

The purpose of *Christianity That Counts* is to call Christians to be engaged by the gospel in ways that transcend a subjectivist, self-centered, and psychologized piety. Christianity is far greater than that. Jesus is Lord over all. As the great Dutch statesman and theologian Abraham Kuyper put it, "There is not a thumb's width of creation over which Christ does not say 'Mine.'" Christ the King has all authority in heaven and on earth (Matt. 28:18); and he calls his disciples to radical obedience as his earthly stewards and kingdom emissaries.

In recent years many scholars have alerted us to the "culture wars" raging over which world views will authoritatively order, reform, and discipline our nation's sensibilities and institutions. All too often Christians who have entered the public battlefield have failed to arm themselves with truth, wisdom, humility, and love. My hope is that these essays and reviews, written over the last ten or so years, will equip the reader to discern better the challenges of the modern world, to appreciate the rich resources of Christian truth, and to feel the need to speak the truth in love to our decaying culture. The chapters vary in length and style—many of them were originally published in different kinds of publications. Nevertheless, they all embrace the central theme of developing a Christianity that counts.

Part 1, Christian Truth Today: Foundations, presents key aspects of the Christian world view. The aim of this section is to unfold something of the richness of Christian truth in relation to modern untruths. I explain the rudiments of a "Christian mind," the Christian "meaning of life," the importance of creeds to full-orbed Christian belief, the need for clear and deep thinking in the pulpit, and the historical richness and substance of the Old Testament revelation.

Part 2 addresses several facets of Christian character. It is not enough simply to have a Christian world view: Christian truth must take root in the center of our lives. From the vantage point of the 1990s, we can see that Christian activism in the eighties was sometimes besmirched by bellicosity and triumphalism, a kind of incivility that often unnecessarily alienated its opposition and failed to achieve its stated goals. To counter these kinds of besetting social sins, I endeavor to establish a basic theology of humility as the foundational Christian virtue, and to exhort readers—and myself—to root out pride and cultivate humility. The next chapter applies this virtue to the discipline of Christian apologetics. The next two chapters argue for the indispensability of reading in the development of a Christian mind and for the important distinction between amassing information and gaining a heart of wisdom. Finally, Rebecca Merrill Groothuis argues for the centrality of worship in the life of both the church and the individual Christian.

Various elements of modern culture are put on trial in Part 3. Rebecca and I ask whether Christianity ought to be considered as one of many lifestyles in a pluralistic culture or as salvation on God's terms. The next two chapters confront the challenges of ethical and religious relativism and outline how the Christian claim of truth makes a difference. I then look at the quest for revelation apart from God—such as attempted communication with plants and UFOs— and the supremacy of God's revelation in Christ. The following chapter by Rebecca Merrill Groothuis breaks new ground in outlining pro-life sensibilities and strategies for an age when the law has sinfully turned pro-abortion. The next chapter reflects on the relationship of religion, the arts, and the role of the state in promoting art, objectionable or otherwise. Since sports has become a powerful idol that shapes the character of many Americans, I attempt to unmask this idol in the next chapter. The significance of the Gulf War involved more than a brief and passionate display of patriotism, tragedy, and sensational technology. It raised ethical questions that I address in a discussion of just-war theory.

The remaining chapters scrutinize different aspects of the New Age movement. Although the New Age has lost some of its celebrity sheen in the past few years, its pantheistic-monistic world view continues to insinuate itself into significant areas of Western culture. I find ancient assistance against the New Age in the writings of the second-century, anti-Gnostic apologist, Irenaeus. I then look at the transformation of *New Age Journal* from the countercultural to the mainstream and how this change serves the New Age cause. The next chapter highlights New Age distortions of Jesus and discusses how to respond to them with apologetic savvy. Joseph Campbell's best-selling *The Power of Myth* is the focus of the next chapter, which evaluates Campbell's New Age appeal and the fallacies of his perspective. The final chapter reviews another influential recent best-seller, Vice President Al Gore's *Earth in the Balance,* and finds it lacking in ecological accuracy and biblical discernment.

Evangelistic appeals make up Part 4. These chapters were originally written for readers who were open to New Age ideas. The chapter on the influential Russian mystic G. I. Gurdjieff was part of a tract I handed out over several days at the showing of a film about his early exploits called *Meetings with Remarkable Men.* The chapter on Christmas was written for a secular newspaper that commissioned (but never published) a Christian response to New Age views of Christmas. The next chapter criticizes the popular belief in reincarnation. The final chapter was originally published as an evangelistic booklet for the Christian Broadcasting Network. I hope this material will inspire Christians to understand and utilize their culture for evangelistic purposes. I also hope that non-Christians reading these chapters might be impressed with the truth of Christ and turn their lives over to his care and command.

An annotated bibliography suggests further resources for developing a Christian mind that counts for Christ in a non-Christian world. It also lists important Christian think tanks and activist ministries that help equip the saints for the King's kingdom work.

Part One

Christian Truth Today
Foundations

1

The Christian Mind

Saint Augustine said that a Christian "believes in thinking and thinks in believing." John Stott, a noted evangelical theologian, tells us that at a most primary level "God has revealed himself in *words* to *minds*."[1] That is, we are created to think and communicate *intelligently* with God, unlike "a horse or mule, which have no understanding" (Ps. 32:9). Bearing the image of God (*imago dei*) involves using our intellectual capability to exercise dominion over creation (Gen. 1:26). Part of human uniqueness and distinctiveness is our ability to reason, to respond humanly to all that concerns us, through analysis, reflection, and consideration. Reason cannot be artificially abstracted from the fullness of God's created reality, as if it stood isolated and independent of other aspects of experience. Neither is reason sufficient for all truth; it must be purified and directed by God's revelation through his Spirit. Yet it is vital to our humanness and integral to our selfhood. In the Sermon on the Mount, Jesus encouraged his hearers to think on his words: "See . . . the lilies of the field" (Matt. 6:28). The point of his preaching required intellectual-spiritual digestion, interpretation, and integration.

We are stewards of the total person; therefore the mind should not be bypassed through a bogus "mystical" shortcut or by intellectual sloth. "The mind of the righteous weighs its answer" (Prov. 15:28). A Christian thinks. Jesus said, "Love the Lord your God with all your heart and with all your soul and with all your mind" (Matt. 22:37). The psalmist's meditation (thinking) on God's ways gave him intellectual astuteness: "I have more insight than all my teachers, for I meditate on your statutes" (Ps. 119:99). The mind is an implement of faith.

Granting that our fallenness and sin have uniformly corrupted us, including our minds, the New Testament nevertheless repeatedly proclaims the reality and power of renewed thinking that sees the world rightly by the enablement of the Spirit (Rom. 12:2; Eph. 4:23). The blood of Christ not only washes us from sin but also gives us the mind of Christ (1 Cor. 2:16), to be employed by Christ.

So the Christian mind is a mind obedient to both the Word made flesh and the living, active word of Scripture (Heb. 4:12). It sees reality not through bi-focals—one lens secular, one lens Christian—but through the lens of an integrated world view in Christian focus, which "take captive every thought to make it obedient to Christ" (2 Cor. 10:5).

What is a world view? According to James Sire, an evangelical author and editor of InterVarsity Press, it is "a set of presuppositions (or assumptions) which we hold (consciously or unconsciously) about the basic makeup of the world."[2] In other words, it is our blueprint for reality, the interpretive net we use to catch the facts and understand them. If every thought and every aspect of life is to be under Christ's lordship, we must develop and refine our distinctively Christian world view. This entails more than glibly tossing about jargon that merely expresses an in-group, cliquish attitude; rather, the Christian mind needs to embrace the Christian *philosophy*—which literally means, from the Greek roots, "the love (*philo*) of wisdom (*sophos*)."

The "philosophy" Paul warns Christians against in Colossians 2:8 is an illegitimate world view based not on God's truth but on "human tradition and the basic principles of this world." *Christian* philosophy is rooted in Christ rather than in godless speculation. In the broadest sense of the word, it guards the "faith given once to the saints" (Jude 3), exposes humanistic counterfeits and attacks, and discerns Christian principles for the whole life. "I, wisdom, dwell together with prudence; I possess knowledge and discretion" (Prov. 8:12). Finding knowledge and discretion for our Christian mind requires not that we flee from encountering rival claims to truth—such as naturalism, nihilism, existentialism, Eastern thought—but that we understand them Christianly. An understanding of the Christian world view will enable us to assess rightly and respond to the non-Christian ideas animating our society. Harry Blamires says that a "Christian mind is a mind trained, informed and equipped to handle the data of secular controversy within a framework of reference (world-view) which is constructed of Christian presuppositions."[3]

What are "Christian presuppositions" and how are they helpful? Christian presuppositions are the indispensable pillars of the Christian world view that all biblical Christians assume or presuppose. They serve as a chart of basic doctrine and give us points by which to navigate through the sea of competing world views. As God said through Isaiah, "And wisdom and knowledge shall be the stability of thy times" (Isa. 33:6). As rudiments of discernment, they define the encounter between Christian and non-Christian ideas.

For example, an auto mechanic presupposes that his operating manual will soundly instruct him in repairing a car, that it will furnish the information and the intellectual tools for understanding and rectifying the situation. If the operating manual proves faulty and inapplicable, he will look for another that makes sense out of the situation. In such a case, his presupposition would be challenged and overthrown.

Similarly, a naturalist student of religion who doesn't recognize God's miraculous intervention in history will presuppose that biblical miracles are mythological until she is presented with sufficient contrary evidence and reasoning to challenge and overthrow her antisupernatural presuppositions. This was the case with C. S. Lewis (see his *Surprised by Joy* and *Miracles*).

Christianity challenges non-Christian thought by presupposing that its "operating manual," the Bible, makes sense of reality and fits the facts in a way that no non-Christian operating manual can, and that Christianity alone can remedy individual and corporate disrepair (sin). "Unless the LORD builds the house, its builders labor in vain" (Ps. 127:1; see also Rom. 1:18–23). The importance of Christian (biblical) presuppositions is both apologetic (defending the faith—exposing faulty presuppositions) and evangelistic (spreading the faith—showing God's rectifying truth). The "foolishness of the gospel" (1 Cor. 1:21) in the overall biblical sense lies not in its internal inconsistency, unintelligibility, or unverifiability, but in the radicality of its encounter with non-Christian thought.[4] In challenging human "suppress[ion of] the truth" (Rom. 1:18), the attempt to determine truth and reality in and of themselves apart from God (Hab. 1:7), the gospel offends humans' pride and their misdirected reason (1 Cor. 1–2). Christ crucified, the suffering servant (Isa. 53), is the wisdom of God (1 Cor. 1:24) that challenges the "wisdom" of humans at the deepest level.

In order to understand the Christian/non-Christian encounter we need to look at the presuppositional groundwork for the construction of a world view in general and the Christian world view in particular. Because truth and wisdom, for the Christian, are not mere concepts but are related to a person, Jesus Christ (John 14:6; 1 Cor. 1:30; Col. 2:3), the elements of a Christian philosophy form a living, pulsating nucleus from which we derive our intellectual energy and direction.

Using Sire's book as a guide, we find that a world view must answer these presuppositional questions: 1) What is really real or prime reality? 2) Who is man? What is his origin and destiny? 3) What happens after death? 4) What determines morality? 5) What is the meaning and purpose of history?

Real Reality

The Christian knows the prime or ultimate reality is God, the Creator, Redeemer, Sustainer, and Judge. "Prime reality" does not imply a hierarchy or chain of being wherein the world is "less real" than a god who sits atop the pyramid of being—a recurring theme in mystical pantheism, such as Platonic philosophy and Gnosticism. God's creation is not to be metaphysically demeaned because of any "thinness of being." The triune God differs from his creation not in degree (of being) but in kind. He is uncreated, unchanging, and self-sufficient; creation is created, subject to decay, and dependent on its Creator. He is our reference point for all meaning and understanding (Isa. 26:3), the ultimate authority. He is "infinite and personal (Triune), transcendent and immanent, omniscient, sovereign and good."[5] "Triune" means one God in three persons: Father, Son, and Spirit. The understanding of his attributes gives us the foundation for understanding our relationship to him and our relationship to the rest of creation. He is beyond this world, distinct from it, and not limited to it, yet personally involved in it (to the point of becoming flesh), knowing its every detail with nothing beyond his providential care and control. He is supremely good and above any corruption. He is the Lord; there is none other of equal importance. He is, as Lewis put it, "the fountain of all facthood," and, as the Westminster Confession put it, "the fountain of all being of whom, through whom, and to whom are all things."[6] From him (the Creator) we derive our being (as creatures). The Christian mind must be God-centered and obedient to his inspired and trustworthy Word, the Bible (2 Tim. 3:16).

Meaning for Humans

People are unique because they bear God's own image as his special creation, the masterwork of divine ingenuity (Gen. 1:26; James 3:9). They are more than complex electro-chemical-biological machines to be manipulated (as the naturalist maintains); they are living souls created to exercise dominion over creation for God's glory (Ps. 8).

Yet God's image in people and their holy vocation have been marred by sin. People are fallen. They have rebelled against God by asserting themselves as autonomous and supreme (Gen. 3:5–6). Because of their all-embracing spiritual alienation from God (Rom. 3:23; Isa. 59:2), people are under a deserved curse

(Gen. 3:14–19), multidimensional in its impact and scope. They are alienated from themselves psychologically (Rom. 7:15–24), alienated from their society sociologically (James 4:1–3), and alienated from their environment ecologically (Isa. 24:5–6; Hos. 4:1–3). "Suffering and death," says theologian Helmut Thielicke, "are rifts and breaches in the created world which have been driven into the world structure by the earthquake of original sin."[7]

Miraculously, people and society are redeemable—not through humanistic self-actualization or self-help, but by God's loving, reconciling grace demonstrated in Christ (Col. 1:13). The gospel calls all to repentance, faith, and healing through Christ.

This biblical belief in the sanctity of life is at loggerheads with world views that presuppose that humans have only a socially related worth (sociological) and not a God-related worth (theological). Because God considers each person valuable, the Christian knows there can be no unwanted fetus-developing person (regarding abortion and infanticide) and no useless individual (regarding euthanasia); all are important to God and created in his image. Christian anthropology is connected to theology, for it is God who gives breath, worth, and meaning to man. The Dutch Christian philosopher Herman Dooyeweerd has said, "The question: 'What is man? Who is he?' cannot be answered by man himself. But it has been answered by God's Word-revelation, which uncovers the religious root and center of human nature in its creation, fall into sin, and redemption by Jesus Christ."[8]

After Death

Death is not a nebulous nothingness or nirvana, nor is it an intermission between reincarnations (Heb. 9:27), but rather the doorway to one of two eternities, one in the company of God, the other forever separate from him. At death one's life is laid bare before God. Christ is here either advocate or prosecutor, Savior or Judge. Because Christ has risen from the dead, Christians have historical hope for their resurrection (1 Cor. 15) from the dead.

Moral Standards

Ethics is transcendent (God-centered), derived from his law. Right and wrong are not ultimately based on majority opinion (human-centered) or on pragmatic feasibility (situational ethics) but on God's revealed moral principles. As Os Guinness said, "Christianity isn't true because it works; it works because it's true."

In a fallen world, a Christian's higher allegiance should lead to an ongoing encounter with pseudobiblical or humanistic ethical systems. As in the early church, "we must obey God rather than men" (Acts 5:29). The pulse beat of revelation, and not the Gallup Poll, should stimulate our steps and define our direction. The Christian thirst for justice, truth, and dignity in all areas of life is compelled by the Creator's commands and consummated by his promise: "Blessed are those who hunger and thirst for righteousness, for they will be filled" (Matt. 5:6).

Meaning of History

The meaning and purpose of history lie in the plan and power of God. His ordering of all events is leading to the consummation of his intent for people and the universe. The tragedy of rebellion and the fall is followed by the drama of redemption—God pursuing humans. History is not the meaningless reign of chance or impersonal necessity, but the unfolding of divine government most clearly seen in the invasion of God into time and space in Christ (John 1:18). A brief providential picture encompasses creation, fall, revelation to the Jews, incarnation, life of Christ, crucifixion, resurrection, ascension, Pentecost, second coming, eternal judgment, and eternal kingdom.

In the economy of the Almighty, both the choices of people and the purpose of God find full fruition, yet without God being the author of sin and without human will crippling the divine design. Theologian Donald Bloesch remarks that "this does not compromise God's omnipotence but testifies of it, for only a truly omnipotent living God could be free to realize his purposes in cooperation with the creature. Yet we must add that at the same time he realizes his plan in opposition to the creature and despite the folly and turpitude of the creature. He brings good out of evil and makes human wrath praise Him."[9] Ultimately all history is derived from the will of God.[10]

This summary of the Christian world view provides an "answer structure" for a person's questions about reality, a way of seeing life in God's revealed perspective. And the more closely we think God's thoughts after him with a truly active Christian mind, the better equipped we become to do all to his glory without intellectual compromise.

"Believing in thinking and thinking in believing" is the preoccupation and conviction of the Christian mind. One need not be an "intellectual" to apply the Christian world view concretely to all of life and thus "give a reason for the hope that is in you" (1 Pet. 3:15) to a doubting world. We need to be admonished, as Romans 12:1–2 reminds us, to be renewed in mind, proving what is good, acceptable, and perfect in God's sight.

2

Creeds, Slogans, and Full-Orbed Orthodoxy

In ordinary times we get along surprisingly well, on the whole, without ever discovering what our faith really is. If, now and again, this remote and academic problem is so unmannerly as to thrust its way into our minds, there are plenty of things we can do to drive the intruder away.

—Dorothy Sayers, *The Whimsical Christian*

All Christians must know and believe the basics if they are Christians at all, since "faith comes from hearing the message, and the message is heard through the word of Christ" (Rom. 10:17). To believe is to understand and trust the truth. Yet the world, the flesh, and the devil conspire to trivialize and amputate the full biblical message. Just what is "the faith that was once for all entrusted to the saints" (Jude 3)?

One means to fend off God's comprehensive truth is through sloganeering; we all easily and adroitly wield this weapon. Echoing our sloganizing culture, we sell the faith (and sell it short) with catchy phrases and semantic gimmicks. In "becoming all things to all men" we say that "Christ adds life" or that one should "try God." The gospel is thus reduced to tidy propositions mechanically presented. The bumper sticker, booklet, or lapel pin exhausts our theological depth.

What's happening here? Am I saying that the gospel cannot be simply presented? No. Am I saying that we sometimes become simpletons? Yes.

We must beware of trivializing the gospel, of presenting it in a form that compromises the radicality of its message. If someone is used to seeing or hearing "Coke adds life," he or she will, most likely, understand "Christ adds life" in the same commercial way: Christ is just another consumer item vying for attention. Christ doesn't speak as crucified King, but as a tricky salesman; not as Lord of the universe, but as genius of the slogan. The slogan trivializes the message and suffocates understanding. So we must move beyond the slogan to the creed.

A creed may simply present the gospel without compromising the full message. Do creeds usurp the authority of Scripture? Some traditions say "No creed but the Bible," but it is more accurate to say "No Bible but the Bible" since everyone attempts to simplify and embody the faith in some way. We all carry our creeds with us, but, regrettably, they're often slogans and not creeds at all.

What is a creed? Creeds have been developed through the history of the church to express the truths of Christianity. They are systematic and synoptic miniaturizations of biblical teaching. By "synoptic miniaturizations" I mean that they attempt to encompass in reduced form the basics of Christian doctrine. They are distilled and compacted pronouncements of faith, shaped by the heat of doctrinal controversy and schism. They aim for conformity to God's revelation. Concerning credal exactitude, R. J. Rushdoony has said that "truth is exact and precise, and the slightest departure from the truth is the substitution of falsity for truth."[1]

If God works through his church in history, and if he preserves the integrity of the biblical witness, we have much to learn from the creeds. Theological formulation is vital to a living faith: the Scripture is profitable for sound doctrine (2 Tim. 3:16) and doctrine needs to be expressed credally.

Some people may have never read a creed. But others have read too many. There is no great unity between the Council of Trent (which solidified the Roman Catholic Counter-Reformation's theology) and the Westminster Confession of Faith (which was formulated with an eye toward the problems of Rome). Roman Catholics and Calvinists had (and have) their disagreements. So why worry about the creeds? Who is to judge them? A word from John Warwick Montgomery is helpful:

> I don't believe that the Apostles' Creed was inspired as was the Bible, but it is a much better creed than I could write myself, and I think that it is a much better creed than any theologian that I have ever met could write, and I'll wager that it is a much better creed than *you* could write. Moreover (and this is far more important), I am positive that the Apostles' Creed is absolutely validated by the Holy Scriptures, in the sense that it fully reflects central biblical teaching.[2]

We should respect and learn from "the [credal] faith of our fathers." The Scriptures are the final court of appeal, but scriptural truth may be encapsulated in the creed. The capsules are of varying sizes. The Apostles' Creed is easily memorized and is recited in many churches. The Westminster Confession covers thirty-three separate subjects, including one of my favorite paragraphs (in chap. 3):

> God from all eternity, did, by the most wise and holy counsel of His own will, freely, and unchangeably ordain whatsoever comes to pass: yet so, as thereby neither is God the author of sin, nor is violence offered to the will of the creatures . . .

I find that to be theologically accurate and uncompromising, devotionally stimulating, and philosophically pregnant. It is true and exciting. And if I want to check it against Scripture, I can search out the texts that are footnoted in the Westminster Confession. Scripture judges the creeds.

A slogan-saturated society tempts us to demote the Christian faith to the level of a slogan. When we give in, we freeze our understanding at a commercialized level. We are satisfied with a starvation diet. But the truth of God is rich and full; our orthodoxy is full-orbed and comprehensive. We may credally summarize it without suffocating it with the trivial. We cannot bottle up and mechanically dispense the great truths of our Lord, but we can celebrate our doctrinal inheritance with joy.

3

The Meaning of Life: *No Joke*

More than a few jokes jab at the quest for "the meaning of life," as if the mere idea were a howler. One ridiculously long story recounts a poor soul's arduous search for life's meaning. The climax comes high in rarified atmosphere where an equally rarified sage declares from his mountain lair that "life is a river." Outraged, the weary seeker protests the sage's pronouncement. To this the pundit says, "You mean . . . it isn't?" End of joke. End of quest. Verdict: Life is a joke.

Jokes are all that remain, it seems, for Woody Allen. His film *Hannah and Her Sisters* portrays Woody barking up one metaphysical tree after another following a reprieve from hypochondriacal worries. But all his searching—including an experiment with Roman Catholicism—is ridiculed in the end. Yet we are told to take comfort that we still have Marx Brothers movies.

Sigmund Freud once wrote, "The moment one inquires about the sense or value of life, one is sick." Freud's atheism ripped purpose from the universe: no God, no ultimate meaning of life. Life just *is*. To puzzle over personal purpose is pathological. We can kid about the meaning of life so long as we realize there is none. Such unvarnished nihilism fires the futility of those who "lead lives of quiet [or not so quiet] desperation," in Thoreau's arresting phrase.

Yet such "pathology" is divinely inscribed on the human heart. The joke must be taken seriously. We are religious beings athirst for "the sense or value of life." Psychologist Erich Fromm saw religion as "any group-shared system of thought and action that offers the individual a frame of orientation and an object of devotion. Indeed, in this broad sense of the word no culture of the past or present, and it seems no culture of the future, can be considered as not having religion."[1]

We all serve a master—whether it be money, sex, fame, education, politics, power . . . or Christ. Rather than being a joke, the meaning of life is the central human question that presses in on us in a rushing torrent of urgency, as psychologist Viktor Frankl's findings have shown. For this reason Frankl, a survivor of a Nazi concentration camp, calls his approach *Logo*-therapy or Meaning-therapy. Only those possessing a meaning and purpose beyond themselves, Frankl discovered, had a chance to outduel death in the death camps. Woody Allen wouldn't have lasted.

But how shall we answer this cry for meaning?

Christianity is a religion of meaning, cosmic meaning. Contra Freud and the nihilistic humorists, Christians see the universe as "charged with the grandeur of God," in the words of Gerard Manley Hopkins. Life moves with divine destiny. But how well can modern Christians articulate their "sense or value of life"? Can we spell out our personal and cosmic meaning—why we have been placed on this planet at this time?

Question 1 of the Westminster Shorter Catechism asks: "What is the chief end of man?" It answers: "Man's chief end is to glorify God, and to enjoy him forever." That's our clue. The meaning and purpose (end) of life is theocentric and doxological. It is God-centered (theocentric). He is Lord of all: Creator, Owner, Redeemer, Sustainer, and Judge. It is also praise/worship-oriented (doxological). All our thoughts and actions should be offered as praise to the living God in obedience to his holy law. "[You shall] love the Lord your God with all your heart and with all your soul and with all your mind" (Matt. 22:37). The holy Trinity is, in Fromm's language, our "object of devotion."[2] We see this in three areas.

Regeneration

Rebellious creatures must be reconciled to a holy God. Being degenerate (without the life of God), we must be regenerated to have faith in Jesus Christ, incarnate Meaning itself. Hence, central to our purpose in life is to call people to faith, to evangelize the nations for the glory of God. The purpose of evangelism, though, is not only to rescue souls from hell—though we ourselves burn at the thought of eternal torment—but also to glorify God by spreading the gospel across the face of the earth. This demands theocentric and doxological evangelism. "How beautiful are the feet of those who bring good news" (Rom. 10:15).

Righteousness

Regeneration is only the beginning of the story. Although we are declared righteous in God's sight when regenerated by God's grace, we are also called to conform our attitudes and actions to God's commands, that we may become righteous at heart and in life. As Jesus said, "If you love me, you will obey what I command" (John 14:15). God delights in an obedient heart and life. He's after godly people.

This is what sanctification is all about: we are increasingly transformed into the image of Christ, our Lord. Just as God justified us, he will sanctify us. And it is supremely good for the soul. The "chief end of man" includes "*enjoying* God forever." "Taste and see that the LORD is good; blessed is the man who takes refuge in him" (Ps. 34:8). As we are made more experientially righteous, we become better and better evidence that Christ is worth knowing (John 13:33–35). We become meaning-bearers for those bereft of meaning; we become theocentrically and doxologically outstanding.

But we don't "hunger and thirst after righteousness" ultimately for our own personal growth or for evangelism, but for the glory of God. This is theocentric and doxological sanctification. "Blessed are the pure in heart, for they will see God" (Matt. 5:8).

Restoration

Regeneration is for the glory of God. Personal righteousness is for the glory of God. In fact, all things are to be offered as praise and worship to the living God. All things are to be restored to godly order (Col. 1:15–20). Christian meaning is holistic. All of culture—politics, economics, science, business, art, education— is to be brought into captivity to Christ, the King. This is what the Puritans wisely called "the crown rights of Jesus Christ." You and I are justified and sanctified that we might have dominion over the earth for the glory of God (Gen. 1:26–28; 9:1–7; Ps. 8).

This was the vision of Abraham Kuyper, who said that the "sacred necessity" laid upon him was "that in spite of all worldly opposition, God's holy ordinances shall be established again in the home, in the school, and in the State for the good of the people; to carve as it were into the conscience of the nation the ordinances of the Lord, to which the Bible and Creation bear witness, until the nation pays homage again to God."

The lordship of Christ covers every square inch of creation. As Stephen Charnock put it, God's "dominion flows from the perfection of his essence; since his essence is unlimited, his royalty cannot be restrained." Jesus Christ now has all power and authority (Matt. 28:18), and he has commissioned us to apply his teaching to the whole of life. Legislatures must be infiltrated, judiciaries made just, the poor fed, textbooks changed, novels written, the unborn and infirm protected, Christian schools multiplied. And "the gates of hell will not overcome [the church]" (Matt. 16:18). This is theocentric and doxological restoration. "Your kingdom come, your will be done, on earth as it is in heaven" (Matt. 6:10).

The meaning of life, then, is regeneration, righteousness, and restoration—all for the glory of God. We have all been called to different tasks for Christ's sake (1 Cor. 12; Rom. 12), but we sometimes mistakenly snatch one aspect of life's meaning and divorce it from the rest. Some Christians see evangelism as the end-all of Christianity. But we are regenerated for a purpose: to glorify God in all that we do for him. Yes, we must evangelize; but the babes must grow to maturity. And growing in righteousness (sanctification) should not be a strictly personal or ecclesiastical process. The righteousness of God working within us by the Holy Spirit must be manifested in God's world at all times and in all areas so our light shines publicly. We are cities "[set] on a hill" (Matt. 5:14), not under a hill. That's restoration at work.

But the work of social/cultural restoration is but a "resounding gong or a clanging cymbal" (1 Cor. 13:1–4) apart from personal regeneration and righteousness. C. S. Lewis reminds us: "There have been men . . . who got so interested in proving the existence of God that they came to care nothing of God himself. . . . There have been some who were so occupied in spreading Christianity that they never gave a thought to Christ. . . . Did ye ever know . . . an organizer of charities that had lost all love for the poor: It is the subtlest of all snares."

But how diligently do we seek the kingdom of God? How meaningful is our Christian service? Do we see the meaning of life as all of a piece? Or are we fragmented? The Reformed tradition convinced me that Christians must endeavor to restore culture for Christ by infiltrating education, the media, and everywhere else. But I've sometimes neglected the devotional life— times of solitude and reflection upon God's Word, times of prayer, times of praise. But how can we know the power of God to transform the world without knowing the presence of God personally? How can we obey orders we have never received, please the One whose voice we never hear? The meaning is clearer when the "still small voice" is heard, when the "joy of the LORD is [our] strength" (Neh. 8:10).

We could close no better than to quote Kuyper, who knew well the true meaning of life: "To be irreligious is to forsake the highest aim of our existence, and on the other hand to covet no other existence than for the sake of God, to long for nothing but for the will of God, and to be wholly absorbed in the glory of the name of the Lord, such is the pith and kernel of all true religion."

The joke is on anyone who dares think otherwise.

4

Misology in the Pulpit

Early in my Christian life I sat under the preaching of Dr. Jack MacArthur, who was doing a Sunday night series on non-Christian groups. As a university student trying to find a way to stand for my Christian convictions in a liberal and pluralistic environment, I found the apologetic and theological depth of his messages to be both uplifting and intellectually inspiring. I could take this material and actively apply it on campus and elsewhere. But this kind of intellectual substance is often lacking in the evangelical pulpit because the life of the mind has not taken its rightful place.

The apostle Peter urged his readers that "if anyone speaks, he should do it as one speaking the very words of God" (1 Pet. 4:11). These solemn words of God, spoken by a preacher, apply to all of us but especially to those who fill the pulpits in our churches. Preachers have a sacred duty to be God's mouthpiece for God's people, to be truth-tellers for truth-seekers. But many evangelical preachers are speaking less than "the very words of God" because the sanctified intellect has not been fully engaged for divine purposes.

Misology is a term used by Plato to describe the position of those who despair of reason's ability to discern or demonstrate truth. Misologists dislike and avoid logic because they deem it impotent, just as misanthropes dislike and avoid people because they deem them bothersome. To this, Plato warns in *The Phaedo* that we ought to be "careful of allowing into our souls the notion that there is no health or soundness in any arguments at all." But has misology gotten into the souls of those in the pulpit?

Few preachers would admit to despairing of reason entirely, yet some sermons speak otherwise. Despite some blessed exceptions, not enough sermons carefully develop arguments and explanations based on a sustained scrutiny of biblical materials. Instead, a biblical text is reviewed and illustrated with anecdotes and humorous asides—sometimes only faintly related to matters at hand. The congregation may be left with a vague warm feeling but receives little instruction. This doesn't mean that some truth isn't spoken, but the truth is seldom presented in a rationally compelling manner or in its divine depth or breadth.

I find at least three main reasons for this implicit misology. First, preachers unconsciously adopt the mentality and methodology of entertainment instead of rational exposition. This approach necessarily constricts content, simplifies presentation, and inhibits the intellect in favor of amusement. Things must be kept lively at all costs lest parishioners "turn the channel" in their minds. It's not coincidental that few sermons exceed thirty minutes, the length of the average television program. Second, preachers may labor under the misconception that rational argument is peripheral to biblical instruction. The Spirit blows where it wills and has no obligation to follow the lead of logic; the Spirit applies truth to hearts in a nonrational manner. Third, many who proclaim God's Word fear that richer sermons are too risky. People are not used to them and won't know what to do with them. It is better to hit an easy and common target than to risk hitting a more difficult one. I can understand this worry, but a diet of milk alone can benefit only infants.

As a hungry parishioner, teacher, and pinch-hit preacher, I can sympathize with the preacher's plight. But let me make a few suggestions in order to encourage those who hold the sacred trust to speak "the very words of God" from the pulpit. I hope to also encourage parishioners to expect and request more substance than is normally conveyed.

First, consider this theological justification for rational preaching. As astute theologians such as Carl Henry and R. C. Sproul have eloquently told us, *logos,* the Greek word for "the Word" in the first chapter of John, can just as accurately be translated as Logic or Reason. Whereas pagan philosophers considered the logos as an impersonal principle that ordered the cosmos and kept it from being chaos, the apostle John confounds unregenerate philosophy and declares that the reason, meaning, and value of the universe are to be found in a personal Creator God. Christ himself was the preincarnate Reason of and for the universe and is now the incarnate and risen Reason. Just as it would be absurd for a journalist to disparage writing or an orator to disparage speaking, the disparagement of logic (mis-ology) is hardly fitting for one who confesses the Logos as Lord and Savior. Paul corroborates this when he affirms that in Christ "are hidden all the treasures of wisdom and knowledge" (Col. 2:2–3).

Therefore, it behooves preachers to be daring and to preach rich biblical content in a logical fashion. Instead of adapting sermons to suit the anti-intellectualism of the day, preachers should rebuke the culture by appealing to the intellects of their parishioners. As a seasoned lecturer in things that matter, philosopher Mortimer Adler advises that speakers aim a bit over their audience's head in order to stimulate them. Why bother telling people what they already know so well? He gives good advice to preachers: "Always risk talking over their heads! By the emotional fervor of your speech, by its physical energy and your manifest bodily involvement with materials that are obviously abstract, you should be able to get them to stretch their minds and reach up for insights they did not have before."[1]

Adler claims that the Great Books of the Western World, which he has done so much to propagate, are always over everyone's head because of their perennial profundity. "This is why," he says, "they are endlessly rereadable as instruments from which you can go on learning more and more on each rereading."[2] How much more is this true of the Holy Scriptures, the greatest book of all, the very words of God? We must "reach up" in order to grow in our knowledge of the truth. If preachers don't provide this intellectual challenge they do a disservice to both the book they love and the congregations they serve.

But sermons that engage the sanctified intellect need not be stuffy affairs devoid of passion or humor. If preaching is, as Phillips Brooks tells us, "truth through personality" then the whole person can honor the depths of divine truth. Jesus, the master preacher, never lacked depth or profundity in his preaching; yet his messages were filled with warmth, a common touch, and even humor, as Elton Trueblood brings out in his classic book *The Humor of Christ.* A cool head goes quite well with both a warm heart and a ready wit.

Sermons are not academic addresses, and the pulpit is the worst place in the universe to exhibit egotistically one's intellect. Nevertheless, I believe that the people of God—with a little cognitive coaching—are able to understand and apply a deeper level of truth than they are accustomed to hearing. Two examples bear this out, one from the university and one from the church.

I taught a course a few years ago called "Christianity, Modernity, and the New Age." This was an accredited class through the experimental college at a state university that allowed me to articulate a Christian response to the New Age movement. Part of the class entailed explaining the biblical world view, which involved a theological and philosophical analysis of the Christian view of God, humanity, ethics, salvation, and history in relation to New Age claims. After the last class a student gave me a letter I'll never forget. She was a Christian who had struggled in her faith after her first pregnancy had miscarried. But through the knowledge she gained in the class about the nature of God and apologetics, she was able to better honor him and trust him as her sovereign and loving Lord. She thanked me for this revelation. I thanked the Lord for this opportunity.

I want to underscore that the lectures on Christianity were not homiletical. I was behind a lectern, not a pulpit, so I could not preach as I would in a church. Nevertheless, the sheer intellectual substance about the nature of God and the reasonableness of Christianity helped change this student's life. Although I taught little more than basic theology—which she had not heard from the pulpit, I presume—her encounter with living truth helped heal her. If theological truth can have this kind of effect in the academic setting, what can it do in the pulpit?

I know of a man who was asked to preach a guest sermon on the New Age movement at a large evangelical church not known for the intellectual substance of its sermons. The guest preacher expounded basic Christian doctrines in relation to the heresies of pantheism, relativism, and reincarnation. He also engaged in apologetics in order to discredit these irrational falsehoods. Although he preached about fifteen minutes longer than the congregation was accustomed to, only a few people left early, no one fell asleep, and almost none of the five hundred in attendance appeared to change channels. I submit that if given the chance this congregation would have responded similarly on a weekly basis.

In *The Soul Winner,* Charles Spurgeon, the great nineteenth-century English preacher, lamented over preachers who were all fire and no light, and who too soon began to preach about what they hardly understood themselves. He urged preachers to fill their sermons with truth about the fall, the law, human nature, Jesus Christ, the Holy Spirit, the everlasting Father, the new birth, obedience to God, and how we learn it. I would add to this list: truth about apologetics and truth about the great social issues of the day such as abortion, homosexuality, race relations, sexual ethics, and our duties to the dispossessed. Christians need intellectual ammunition as well as subjective passion if they are to face a hostile world with biblical integrity. Let's consider in more detail the area of apologetics in preaching.

My observation in numerous churches over the years is that apologetics is usually not welcome in the evangelical pulpit. The gospel is proclaimed, but seldom defended in such a way as to resolve the doubts of the faithful or to answer the objections of the sceptic. Sermons traffic in truths largely unrooted in rational reflection; preachers often deem such cerebral fare either unnecessary or impossible. But despite its rarity in the pulpit (and elsewhere), the rational defense of Christianity as objectively true is both necessary and possible.

It is necessary because the very idea of objective, universal, and absolute truth is eroding in pluralistic America. In *What Americans Believe,* George Barna reports that only 28 percent of his respondents expressed a strong belief in "absolute truth." Religion is then viewed as just another personal and subjective choice among innumerable other choices facing American individualists. Such relativists need to be convinced that Christianity is more than just a "lifestyle" or a "religious preference," if they are to surrender to Christ as "the way and the truth and the life" (John 14:6).

In our pluralistic culture sermons should set forth the exclusive claims of Christ as rationally superior, not just dogmatically demanding. This means building a reasonable case for the uniqueness and finality of the incarnation that can withstand critical questions: Are the biblical documents reliable? Is Christ significantly different from other religious figures? Can't the pagan be saved? Aren't miracles fables? Isn't God in everyone? As preacher and apologist Francis Schaeffer taught us, "honest questions deserve honest answers," not a rejection of the questions. We should remember that although Schaeffer is best remembered as an apologist, his apologetic ministry grew out of his desire to pastor and evangelize those immersed in modern culture. May his example inspire us to do the same. Relevant preaching demands that the sceptical questions of the day be recognized and responded to in the pulpit.

Besides the practical and contemporary necessity, the Scriptures themselves report people of God contending for "the faith that was once for all entrusted to the saints" (Jude 3). An apologetic for apologetics is that we find apologetics in the Bible itself, often mingled with preaching (see Acts 17:16–31). The preacher Peter gave us this great apologetic charge: "Always be prepared to give an answer to everyone who asks you to give the reason for the hope that you have. But do this with gentleness and respect" (1 Pet. 3:15).

F. F. Bruce's insightful book, *The Defense of the Gospel in the New Testament,* bears witness to the various strategies required by the early church to defend the faith amidst the task of proclaiming it. He says, "The men and women who condemned the gospel in the first century 'had understood the times': the kingdom of God calls loudly for such men and women today."[3]

It is not only necessary but also possible for pastors to preach apologetics in the pulpit. Whatever their level of formal training in apologetics, preachers can benefit from studying the relevant books, both ancient and modern, that intellectually advance Christianity. For instance, Blaise Pascal's *Pensées* is a neglected masterpiece that repays careful study. Pastors who take up apologetics will deepen their own spirituality by growing in their understanding of Christian truth, how it can lose credibility, and how it can be defended afresh by drawing on both ancient and modern resources.

Considering the demands on pastors, no one should require they become apologetic wizards. But given the severity of the need, the apologist G. K. Chesterton's quip should be heeded: "Anything worth doing is worth doing badly." Although his quip may not apply to brain surgery, feeding the starving with something less than gourmet cuisine is no crime. A pastor need not have a Ph.D. in New Testament studies to give a defense of the New Testament as historically reliable. Nor does one need an advanced degree in philosophy to say something intelligent about the perpetually vexing problem of evil or whether the Bible is rational.

The preaching of apologetics has two direct benefits. First, the doubting believers in the congregation (often the most thoughtful people) will find that doubt can be erased, if not resolved, because there are reasons to believe. Many in our congregations are praying, "Lord, I believe, but help my unbelief." Apologetics helps answer that prayer. Great doubts, honestly encountered and mastered, can lead to even greater faith.

Second, the preaching of apologetics will challenge unbelievers with arguments and evidence. Instead of simply hearing about Christianity or being urged to accept it, they will receive rational arguments to support it. In a culture that holds Christianity in intellectual contempt, a good deal of pre-evangelism (apologetics) is required before evangelism will stick. Imagine the surprise of the unbeliever who stumbles into a church on Easter to hear a compelling defense of the resurrection of Jesus as an objective fact of history! Instead of hearing only "He is risen!" he hears, "This is why you should believe he is risen!" Or think of the possibilities of a Christmas sermon that not only explains the meaning of the season but also answers common objections that the virgin birth is nothing but a myth.

We should grant that the Holy Spirit often works in ways beyond our rational comprehension (Isa. 55:8–9) and that we should never count on bare logic to convert or to edify a soul. Yet this statement only undermines the idea that logic is sufficient in the pulpit; it does nothing to undermine the necessity of logic in the pulpit. God says, "Come now, let us reason together" (Isa. 1:18). Biblical preaching certainly requires more than arguments and factual presentation; it must exhort if it is to convey the "very words of God" with power, but exhortation without argumentation is hollow, just as argumentation without exhortation is vain . . . and mere amusement with neither argument nor exhortation is worst of all.

The most effective kind of exhortation is built on truths reasonably presented. The order of exposition should be

1. This is God's truth.
2. This is why we believe it.
3. This is how to put it into practice.

We are more likely to listen to and obey the recommendations of our physician if he has reasonably explained and defended his description of our condition. If we find his diagnosis reasonable we are more likely to follow his prescription. Likewise, the preaching of reasonable conclusions is far more powerful than preaching mere assertions or opinions unsupported by explanation and argumentation, no matter how vociferously they may be urged upon us.

Until more rational conclusions find their way into our sermons, misology will continue its silent siege on truth; we will continue to find more fire than light in our pulpits; and congregations that should be rich in God's revealed truth will remain intellectually impoverished. But through prayer, repentance, and education the Spirit of truth may again fill our pulpits with "the very words of God." The dignity of that platform demands nothing less.

5

Hebrew History
in the Ancient World

Modern ears are often assailed by voices claiming that all religions teach the same essential truths and equally lead to God, however differently God may be defined or explained. Yet in turning to the Hebrew sacred Scriptures we find a view of God's action in history quite different from that of ancient Israel's religious neighbors. The God of the Hebrews is a God who makes a difference in space-time history; and because of this, his mighty historical acts are worthy of historical record. The writers of the Old Testament were not content to parrot the mythologies of pagan imagination. Their history writing was rooted in truths revealed on the dramatic stage of history.

The aim of this chapter is to outline the distinctives of ancient Israel's historiography as witnessed in the Hebrew Scriptures that have become the canonical Old Testament of the Bible. Some reference will be made to the historiography (or lack thereof) of the surrounding Near Eastern cultures for purposes of juxtaposition.

We will first look at Israel's historiography as a whole, cutting a wide swath rather than focusing on particular issues or aspects of their history or historiography. Second, we will not engage in the various critical controversies considering the exact date and authors of the Hebrew Scriptures, although we will consider some of the motivations behind biblical criticism. Third, because our interest is historiographical, we will focus on the portions of the Old Testament that more directly relate to history rather than concerning ourselves with wisdom literature (Proverbs, Ecclesiastes, Song of Solomon) and Psalms (although these will be shown as not lacking in historical content).

What Is Historiography?

Historiography literally means "the writing of history." Thus the historiographer is a historian, one who records past events for present and future attention. But historiography may also refer to the history of historiography; that is, to the study of how and why various historians wrote history as they did. The "why" concerns philosophical or theological historiography; the "how" concerns the method of historiography (choice of subject matter or interpretation).[1] So when we look to Israel's historiographic tradition we will consider the reason for recording historical events (philosophical/theological historiography) and how those events were recorded (methodological historiography).

Having defined historiography, let us define "history" itself. Many definitions may be given, but for our purposes history is defined as the actual space-time events of the past. It is the subject matter of historiography (however faithful or unfaithful the particular historiography may be to history itself). Thus the Hebrew "sense of history" refers to their understanding of the space-time events of the past. For our purposes, history will be juxtaposed with myth, with myth being understood as an imaginative story that is not meant to be an actual historical record of space-time events. In comparing Israel's historiography with other nations the main point is made that Israel was concerned with space-time events rather than myths.

Much more material seems to exist on Israel's theology[2] of history than on methodological historiography. Although more material on methodological historiography would be appreciated, the material on theological historiography is crucial because the view of history and the writing of it fit together. What is written and how it is written will reveal a theology of history; and the theology of history will greatly determine how that history is written. It seems safe to say that theology of history exists before any history is written but that the theology of history also grows out of what is written as later writers reflect upon it.

What Made the Hebrews Different?

Several aspects of ancient Hebrew historiography distinguish it from other Near Eastern peoples' historiography. First, some of their writings have been referred to by Harry Barnes as "the earliest appearance of the true historical narrative of which any record has anywhere been preserved."[3] Barnes also notes that "with the exception of the Hebrew historians, ancient oriental literature was slight and informal until very late times"[4] when it was influenced by Hellenistic Greek culture. The nature of this writing was "royal propaganda" that glorified kings by reciting their military, hunting, or architectural exploits. These writings were probably written by priest-scribes but were attributed to the monarchs or the gods. They were "propaganda" in that they lacked a critical sense. Their sole purpose seemed to be to glorify the monarch.[5] Herbert Butterfield adds that most of the historical writing during this time "had been mere dips into the past for the purpose of showing the monarch of the moment had removed the evils which had existed under his predecessors or had broken previous records. For the rest, the effective 'past' was the world of epic poetry, and behind that, the realm of pure mythology."[6] The eighteenth-century philosopher of history Johann Gottfried von Herder comments that the Hebrew writings were "advantageously distinguished" as history from the previous historical writings in that "they neither derived their account from hieroglyphics, nor obscured by them; for it [their history] is taken merely from family chronicles, and interwoven with historical tales or poems; and its value as history is evidently increased by this simplicity of form. This account, too, derives singular weight from its having been preserved for some thousands of years, with almost superstitious scrupulosity, as a divine prerogative of the race."[7] With the Hebrews we find what Butterfield calls one of the greatest surprises in the whole historical story: "a people not only supremely conscious of the past but possibly more obsessed with history than any other nation that has ever existed."[8]

Before outlining the nature of Israel's historical writing in more detail, some explanation will be given as to why other Near Eastern peoples lacked the historical interest of the Hebrews.

The Other Gods and History

The Hebrew writings themselves reveal a God radically different from the gods recorded in Mesopotamian, Hittite, Egyptian, and Persian literature. The God of the Old Testament is not continuous with humanity and nature. He stands transcendent as Creator and Lord of all creation, though he is not removed from the affairs of his world.[9] Other oriental views of deity were essentially pantheistic/monistic: God, humanity, and nature were all of a piece, an inseparable whole. Political philosopher Eric Voegelin saw Israel as having history as its "inner form"; other Near Eastern societies were based on cosmological myth that viewed society as embedded in the cyclical processes of the natural order.[10] Biblical scholar Michael Fishbane comments that "in this [pantheistic/monistic] world-view, the gods are immanent and near, and there is a deep harmony linking man and god and world. This harmony is truly ontological."[11] Because any object or person is potentially revelatory, anything may become an idol to be worshiped. In Egypt, for example, "the god of creation (Atum) was identified with the lizard, and the sun-god (Ra) with a dung beetle."[12] The focus of concern in these cultures was more with nature/God/humanity than history per se.

Israel's God and History

Israel, on the contrary, saw a radical distinction between Creator and creation. The Decalogue (Ten Commandments) prohibits idolatry of all kinds (Exod. 20:4–6). Although the God of the Hebrews reveals himself in natural processes (cf. Ps. 19:1, "the heavens declare the glory of God"), he is not limited to them or identified with them (for example, see Isa. 40:6–31). He is not, then, like other oriental deities, a nature god tied to the pattern of the seasons. Rather, he intervenes in history from above. As Mircea Eliade has repeatedly pointed out, most ancient cultures viewed the cosmos as a process of ever-reoccurring events mirroring in some way the divine order (or archetypes). Assuming that the uniqueness of Israel's thought was a later development than other oriental thought, Eliade says that with Israel

> for the first time, we find affirmed, and increasingly accepted, the idea that historical events have a value in themselves, insofar as they are determined by the will of God. This God of the Jewish people is no longer an Oriental divinity, creator of archetypical gestures, but a personality who ceaselessly intervenes in history, who reveals his will through events (invasions, sieges, battles, and so on). Historical facts thus become "situations" of man in respect to God, and as such they acquire a religious value that nothing had previously been able to confer on them.[13]

Eliade sees the Hebrew view of history as "the epiphany of God."[14] Because God is emancipated from nature, he is free to act as he chooses in nature; the Creator is not bound by his creation. Fishbane observes that "history and time are given new meaning as the expression and mode of manifestation of a god of omnipotent will."[15]

The View of Time

The Hebrew view of time itself is set free from the cycles of nature. As the creation account of Genesis declares, the passage of "days" is not dependent on the heavenly bodies (which are not created until the fourth day). Here again we see the differences between the Hebrew and the surrounding views. Any notion of sun or star worship or astrological control of the stars and planets over humanity (popular in the surrounding oriental cultures)[16] is dispelled. They are rather created servants of God (Gen. 1:14–18). James Muilenburg, in a lengthy essay on the Hebrew view of time, comments that

> in Israel the mystery and meaning of time is not resolved by appeal to the cosmic world of space; among the other nations the heavenly bodies are deified and *chronos* spatializes time into extension and duration. In the one, time is grasped in terms of purpose, will, and decision; in the other the secrets of the stars are determined by "those who divide the heavens, who gaze at the stars, who at the new moons predict what shall befall you [astrologers]" (Isa. 47:13. Cf. also and especially 44:24ff.).[17]

God's will in history is demonstrated in linear development, not endless repetition. Muilenberg says: "Cyclical views were current in the nature religions of the Near East, but Israel's conception is linear, not a straight line of unilateral development, but one which moved tortuously as history itself."[18]

Uniqueness of Historical Events

The linearity of time also entailed the uniqueness and unrepeatability of historical events. The creation itself as recorded in Genesis is a one-time event at the beginning of history. Gerhard Hasel notes that the Genesis account is set off against the Egyptian view of creation, which sees the "created world's return to a chaotic state." "Egyptian cosmology does not know a once-for-all creation which took place 'in the beginning' as is expressed in Gen. 1:1. It does know of a creation 'in the first time' (*sp tpy*), which, however, is ever repeated in cyclical fashion, in such a way that man himself experiences it."[19] The revelation of the law on Mount Sinai is also viewed as an event without parallel in history. Moses says to the children of Israel: "For ask now of the days that are past, which were before you, since the day God created man upon the earth, and ask from one end of the heaven to the other, whether such a great thing as this has even happened or was heard of? (Deuteronomy 4:32–34)."[20] Heschel comments that Judaism transformed agricultural festivals (tied to seasonal fecundity) into "commemorations of historical events."[21] The spring festivals became Passover, which celebrated the exodus from Egypt; the Feast of Weeks, a wheat harvest festival, was transformed into a commemoration of the giving of the law (Torah) at Mount Sinai; the Feast of Booths, an old festival of vintage, celebrates the dwelling of the Israelites in booths during their wandering in the wilderness before entering the Promised Land (Canaan). Heschel says that "while the deities of other peoples were associated with places or things, the God of Israel was the God of events: the Redeemer from slavery, the Revealer of the Torah, manifesting Himself in events of history rather than in things or places."[22]

Stability for History

The biblical view of God also provided stability for history. Although historical events were understood in terms of God's judgment or blessing, which involved either disaster or prosperity for Israel (and other nations), history was not the whim of gods or the caprice of chaos. The non-Jewish oriental creation accounts often depict creation emerging from chaos with the aid of a god or gods. The primeval Chaos remains a threat to nonomnipotent gods and humanity. But the Genesis creation account records no struggle between God and Chaos as do the Babylonian, Hittite, Phoenician, or Egyptian accounts.[23] The upshot for the Hebrew view of history is that history is steered from on high; it is not in a state of fluctuation due to cosmic power struggles that are ultimately irresolvable. Butterfield notes that with the polytheism of the ancient Near East, "the destinies of men hung precariously on the whims of an assembly." He also mentions that the ancient Sumerians had no sense of historical continuity between past and present: "history to them would be in the range of what we might regard as mere happening." Only the "caprice of the gods decided the various turns of fortune."[24] Without going into detail with regard to Mesopotamian, Egyptian, or other views it should be noted, as C. F. Whitley points out, that the "Hebrew view of history in which events are conceived as cohering in a purposeful whole is not characteristic of other Near Eastern cultures."[25] The other nations lacked the Hebrew's sense of *telos* or purpose. James Orr comments on the teleological sense of the Hebrew's view of history: "Its history . . . is dominated by the idea of purpose. It is this which gives unity to the history and to the books which contain it."[26] The Hebrew view of history and time thus made the recording of historical events important and even necessary for national identity, as we will see.

Messianic Expectation

In addition to the purposeful and linear concept of history, the Hebrew Scriptures, particularly the prophets, look forward to a time of unsurpassed peace and prosperity brought about by the Messiah, or anointed one. Isaiah 11, for instance, speaks of the Messiah who "with righteousness . . . will judge the needy" and with "justice . . . will give decision for the poor of the earth. He will strike the earth with the rod of his mouth; with the breath of his lips he will slay the wicked. Righteousness will be his belt and faithfulness the sash around his waist" (Isa. 11:4–5). This Messiah will inaugurate a period of peace in which "the wolf will live with the lamb, the leopard will lie down with the goat, the calf and the lion and the yearling together; and a little child will lead them" (11:6). William Dyrness points out that "the messianic future" brings together several Old Testament historical themes such as the perfection of the garden of Eden and Adam's perfect relationship with God (Amos 9:13; Ps. 72:16); of a deliverance similar to that of Moses from Egypt (Hos. 2:14–23); and it proclaims a future kingship even greater than David's. "[T]he imagery of the shoot from the stump of Jesse (Is. 11:1, 10), that is the remnant of the house of David, is the most familiar image of the Messiah. The Messiah is a son of David (Ps. 2:7), seated at the Lord's right hand (Ps. 110:1) and is himself divine (Ps. 45:6)."[27]

Much more could be said here, but the salient point for historiography is that the Hebrew writers looked ahead to a future blessing brought about by a future Messiah promised to Israel and all the earth.

We will now turn more specifically to the nature of the Hebrew historiography in the hope of capturing its spirit (rather than specifically enumerating all its characteristics).

Hebrew Historiographic Distinctives

Butterfield stresses what he calls "the originality of the Hebrew scriptures" in his *Origins of History*. He notes that the sense of "historical memory" is essential to the Hebrews.[28] They were a people delivered from Egypt's bondage and solidified by the hand of God working in history. Even the genres of the Old Testament that are not primarily concerned with history (such as apocalyptic, poetry, and wisdom literature) still reflect upon the significance of God's acts in history. The Psalms, for example, often lament that God's people have forgotten God's mighty, saving deeds of the past and so have strayed from him. Psalm 103 says, "Praise the LORD, O my soul, and forget not all his benefits . . . The LORD . . . made known his ways to Moses, his deeds to the people of Israel" (vv. 2, 6–7). Remembering the mighty acts of God was essential for Hebrew faith, as the religious festivals point out. This "historical memory" kept them united as a people.

Historical Narrative and Ethics

Historical narrative is therefore crucial in Hebrew historiography. God's acts in history were recorded for posterity. And ethical motivation for the people of Israel was tied to historical remembrance. Butterfield notes that the narrative of Israel's beginnings with their father Abraham, their growth as a people in Egypt, and their exodus from Egypt "so imprinted itself on their minds that when, at a later date, they were inclined to ask them-selves why they ought to obey the commandments they could think of no better statement of the reason. Instead of resorting to ethical discourse of philosophical speculation, they appealed once again to history."[29] Thus Moses tells the Hebrews that when their sons will someday ask the meaning of the law they should remind them of their history of bondage and liberation (Deut. 6:20–23). Joshua's challenge to his people to obey God and not the pagan gods is also couched in historical memory. In light of God's previous faithfulness his people should serve him alone (Josh. 24:2–15). Butterfield says that these pieces of history "per-formed also for them the function that was performed by the epic in the case of other people."[30] In fact, it may have outperformed the functions performed by the epic because of the nature of Israel's view of history. History solidified them as a people, giv-ing them a sense of destiny, responsibility, and purpose. Butter-field comments that Israel's sense of history "seemed to relieve this people of the necessity of having an elaborate mythology. Religion became profoundly involved with history instead."[31]

Covenantal Promise

Israel's God was involved in history according to the promise made to his people that they would "possess the land." Butter-field says that "it seemed that the whole history of the people had been a history based on the Promise."[32] The entire structure of the Old Testament canon is covenantal (relating to God's promise and command and the human response): God (as supreme Suzerain) making a treaty with his people that involved blessings for obedience to the covenantal law and cursing for disobedi-ence. In fact, portions of Deuteronomy and elsewhere closely resemble the treaty documents of other Near Eastern nations (but also differ in their theistic—not polytheistic—formulation, among other things).[33] This promise and its stipulations were ethically qualified, and thus the Hebrews historical writing takes on a markedly ethical character.

Ethical Evaluation

Christopher J. H. Wright notes that the historical narrative showed the Hebrew historian's ethical consciousness: "They performed the task of collecting, selecting, editing, and commenting on the stories of Israel's past—centuries of it—with consistent theological and ethical criteria and assessment. They were prepared to evaluate boldly events and people in a way that affirmed the ethical significance of both." Wright says, though, that the Hebrew historian did not always "moralize" in obvious ways, but often left the reader to draw his or her own conclusions. Yet the ethical element remains because God is viewed as working through "the narrative—explicitly or behind the scenes—initiating, reacting, controlling."[34] Unlike the "court histories" of the surrounding nations, the record of King David, for example, "shows an amazing impartiality and independence, and could hardly have been produced by the king himself or on his behalf"[35] because of its realistic portrayal of his weaknesses as well as his strengths. David is not only brave in battle, but also immoral in his affair with Bathsheba. The writers don't hide his imperfections or excuse them.

Barnes notes that "the Books of Kings were the first practical illustration of the notion of history as 'philosophy teaching' by example. The author sought primarily to convince this people of the value of religious fidelity by citing historical illustration of the disasters that had come to the Hebrews because they deserted their national religion."[36] In Old Testament theology kings—as well as the rest of humanity—were sinners before a holy God. This is in contradistinction to the view of kingship in the surrounding nations. The Old Testament historians are not therefore afraid to depict them as fallible. This evaluative historiography is also seen in the prekingdom days of the judges (recorded in the Book of Judges). The judges and people are portrayed as either serving or disobeying God—with the consequence of either blessing or cursing.

Kline points out that the post-Pentateuchal books emphasize the convenantal and ethical relationship between God and Israel: "The narratives rehearse the continuing benefits bestowed by Yahweh [God] as a faithful Protector of his vassal kingdom"[37] and thus retain the theme of the historical prologue of the treaty documents (law codes) of Israel. Just as the treaty documents of Deuteronomy emphasize God's deliverance of Israel from Egypt, so too these books "relate how he [God] staffed their ranks with judges and kings, priests and prophets, for the development of the kingdom after the pattern that had been prescribed in the constitutional stipulation of the Pentateuch." But Kline mentions that the Old Testament's "historiography pursues the countertheme of Israel's repeated covenant breaking and the consequent affliction on them of the evils delineated beforehand in the curse sanctions of the Mosaic treaties, particularly in Deuteronomy [especially Deut. 8:11–20; 28:15–68]."[38] Old Testament scholar Martin Noth comments that Israel's narrative tradition was tied to the view of God's laws "as a collection of historical examples of the attitude of man to the law and its consequences."[39]

Universal History

Butterfield points out that non-Hebrew historiography of the Near East sometimes recorded events and tried to interpret them, even in some cases in moral terms, as with the Hittites.[40] Yet the Hebrew writings show a distinctive logic of continuity, of promise and fulfillment according to God's control of history. Butterfield says, "In Mesopotamia there was a notion of destiny, but even this had no logic or continuity." Neither did it have an "overarching theme."[41] Hebrew historiography, on the other hand, introduces a "large scale interpretation"[42] of history that includes not only Israel's origins and destiny, but that of the whole world. We find, then, a sense of "universal history," a history that encompasses—at least in principle—all people and places.[43]

The Book of Genesis shows the origin of the universe and all of earth's peoples, starting with Adam and Eve and moving through their descendants, both the people of promise (covenant) and other nations. Throughout the Old Testament, other nations are spotlighted. The Assyrians are seen as instruments in God's hands (Isa. 10:7); the Egyptians were also seen as within God's plan (Isa. 31:3); Nebuchadnezzar, although not partaking in the covenant, is portrayed as a servant of God (Jer. 25:9; 32:26); the same held for Cyrus, conqueror of the Lydians and Babylonians (Isa. 45:1–13). Other examples could also be given.

Although Hebrew historians viewed Israel as God's chosen nation, this did not restrict their historical vision. All peoples and nations were seen under the lordship of God. They were not viewed as incidental to history. The prophets, for instance, showed a great concern not only for Israel's moral standing before God, but the moral standing of other nations as well. Heschel notes that "the prophet may be regarded as the first universal man in history; he is concerned with, and addresses himself to all men."[44] Jeremiah, for instance, says: "From early times the prophets who preceded you and me have prophesied . . . against many countries and great kingdoms" (Jer. 28:8). The prophets often recorded the history of the nations they prophesied against. Judgment was announced because of historical misdeeds. Amos thundered against Damascus, Gaza, Tyre, Edom, Ammon, and Moab in addition to warning Israel and Judah (Amos 1:3–2:6), citing their historical acts as the justification for judgment: "For three sins of Damascus, even for four, I will not turn back my wrath. Because she threshed Gilead with sledges having iron teeth, I will send fire upon the house of Hazael that will consume the fortresses of Ben-Hadad" (Amos 1:3–4). Heschel nicely summarizes the prophetic view: "[With the prophets] was born the idea of one history. The particular event or situation is related to Him Who rules over all nations. Just as the knowledge of nature was born with the discovery of principles determining all happenings in nature, so is consciousness of history the result of an awareness of One God judging all events in history."[45]

Critical Issues

Butterfield believes that the Hebrews' sense of universal history gave impetus to the writing of universal history ever since, and marked an advance over previous more parochial views of history.[46] Nevertheless, some studies of historiography omit any reference to ancient Israel. Much of this attitude stems from the modern disbelief in the miraculous that is an integral part of the Old Testament writings (the parting of the Red Sea, the manna from heaven, the giving of the law). This is in large measure a philosophical issue that will not be settled here, but it is important to look at the Old Testament documents in terms of what their original authors intended to say. The miraculous stories are not written as imaginative fantasy but, rather, as factual history. They do not have the aura of the epic or tribal myth. In addition, Israel's theology of history itself radically differs from that of the surrounding nations. Their God is a God of history who acts in history and wants his people to remember his acts in history. History, and the writing of history, took on a new meaning for the nation of Israel.

Much of modern biblical criticism that attempts to ascertain when, where, and how the Old Testament books were written— and concludes that the biblical record is not to be trusted as it stands—often engages in questionable historical speculations. This can be seen, to some extent, in Butterfield's approach also. The (antisupernaturalist) philosophical presupposition that, for example, predictive prophecy is not possible may influence how the critics date the Old Testament books. Further, variation in style and content in the Old Testament books leads many critics to postulate many authors and changes over time. Suffice it to say that these conclusions are speculative and often receive an acceptance incommensurate with their plausibility. More conservative scholars have maintained earlier dating of the Old Testament books, their historical accuracy, the reality of the miraculous, and predictive prophecy.[47]

But despite disagreement, the student of Hebrew historiography finds a rich source of historical material generated by a people steeped in a profoundly historical consciousness. Their God was a God active in history, the Lord of linear history, the ethical judge of history, and the one whose acts demanded historical record and reflection.

Part **Two**

Christian Character

6

Humility
The Heart of Righteousness

Writing about humility is a humbling experience. I write with both reluctance and a sense of daring—and I hope without presumption. I am reluctant because I am no expert in the matter and do not want to speak too far beyond my experience. Nevertheless, I dare to proceed because I have been brought to see that humility is the living center of the Christian life, the indispensable heart of righteousness. As Andrew Murray said, "Humility is the only soil in which the graces root; the lack of humility is the sufficient explanation of every defect and failure. Humility is not so much a grace or virtue along with others; it is the root of all, because it alone takes the right attitude before God, and allows Him as God to do all."[1] Christian spirituality is founded upon humility of spirit and cannot live without it.

No matter what our gifts may be—teaching, preaching, writing, organizing, counseling, leading—and no matter how expertly we exhibit them, they are hauntingly hollow without humility. Without humility, others may hear of Christ from us, but they will not see him in us. He will remain more of a rumor than a reality.

If we want Christ to become a public reality in us, we should seek to understand what humility is and how to cultivate it.

Things valuable and rare, such as money and precious stones, are often counterfeited, and so humility is counterfeited by inept imitators. Someone who publicly bemoans his inadequacies with predictable regularity is probably not humble. He is, rather, disgusted with himself and seeking to have others build him up. Nor does humility consist in perpetually pondering the somber and unpleasant. Dour souls, forever solemn and glum, are probably too wrapped up in melancholy to be meek.

We could expose other imposters. But although counterfeits should be unmasked, they can provide no solid food for humility; one can avoid poison and still not know what makes for manna. The manna of humility can be understood as based on two doctrinal pillars known to us all: that we are creatures of the Creator, and we are redeemed by Christ the Redeemer.

Humility is a condition of the heart in which a person is disposed to receive all good things as a bestowal of grace. The humble refuse to take credit where it is not due, and recognize that "every good and perfect gift is from above, coming down from the Father of the heavenly lights" (James 1:17). Humility is based on our relationship with God. We are humble before God as a result of apprehending who God is in relation to who we are.

Humility as Creatures

Humility is rooted not only in our being rescued from sin by the Savior; it is equally rooted in our position as creatures of the Creator. We are not the source of our own existence or of any good that greets us. All is a gift from another—the thunderous rush of the surging waves of the ocean, the luminous smile of a wife or a husband, a good night's sleep, a moonlit night, a child's laughter. All is received by mere mortals. Adam and Eve in all their unfallen splendor owed worship and thanksgiving to their Maker. As do we.

It is a short step from thanksgiving to humility; conversely, it is quite a strain to be thankful and prideful at one sitting. Thanksgiving lifts us out of ourselves and into the graces of another where we find joy in the recognition of goodness bestowed. We are the recipients, not the Benefactor. As Murray put it: "But as God is the ever-present, ever-active One, who upholdeth all things by the word of his power, and in whom all things exist, the relation of the creature to God could only be one of unceasing, absolute, universal dependence."[2]

While a reflection on this dependence naturally triggers thanksgiving and worship, pride is rooted in ingratitude and claims for itself what it can never merit. The Book of Acts tells of the pride of Herod who, after an ostentatious public address, was lauded by his subjects as a god: "Immediately, because Herod did not give praise to God, an angel of the Lord struck him down, and he was eaten by worms and died" (Acts 12:21–23). Although God rarely judges so quickly, pride itself eats away at those who are intent on promoting themselves. Pride deems that no promotion is ever good enough, no accomplishment satisfactory, and no victory final. When we try to fill ourselves with ourselves we remain empty—if noisy. As Blaise Pascal put it regarding our need for grace, "this infinite abyss can be filled only with an infinite and immutable object; in other words by God himself."[3]

Saved by Humility

Humility is not only the appropriate response of dependent creatures, but also the Christian's invaluable inheritance in Christ. Our salvation was achieved through humility and for humility. Humility was the instrument of redemption. Christ did not consider equality with God something to be grasped; instead, he humbled himself in order to serve us and his Father by leaving the perfection of heaven and dying on the cross to set us free from sin (Phil. 2:5–11). It may be difficult to fathom how God incarnate could be humble, but this is only because our vision of humility is clouded. The humility of Christ is rooted in his servant heart. He came not to be served, but to serve, and to give his life as a ransom for fallen people (Mark 10:45).

The measure of Christ's earthly greatness was his obedience to the Father for our sake. He did not seek his own glory, although he deserved it; and he did not insist on his own will, although he could have commanded legions of angels to save him from the cross. Instead of demanding that the disciples kiss his feet, he washed theirs. Instead of slapping Judas at the last supper, he kissed him. Instead of silencing his opponents by summoning fire from heaven, he loved his enemies—even on the cross, asking his Father to forgive them.

We can in this light better understand what Jesus meant when he said, "Come to me, all you who are weary and burdened, and I will give you rest. Take my yoke upon you and learn from me, for I am gentle and humble in heart, and you will find rest for your souls. For my yoke is easy and my burden is light" (Matt. 11:28–30). This is Jesus' explanation of how we can receive his humility. His is the yoke of humility; he above all others was meek before his Father in heaven. And it is this humility that he offers to those who take up his yoke. We will miss the heart of this verse (as I did for years!) unless we see that Jesus both exemplifies and offers humility. Humility is a primary benefit of salvation. If we understand the terms of our salvation, our only response can be humility. One who is redeemed by the grace of God has no cause for boasting. As Paul announced, "For it is by grace you have been saved, through faith—and this not from yourselves, it is the gift of God—not by works, so that no one can boast" (Eph. 2:8–9).

Pride is excluded in principle from first to last. As Jeremiah said, "Let not the wise man boast of his wisdom or the strong man boast of his strength or the rich man boast of his riches, but let him who boasts boast about this: that he understands and knows me, that I am the LORD, who exercises kindness" (Jer. 9:23–24).

If we understand the gospel and know who we are in Christ, we can trust the kindness of God himself instead of pridefully seeking the flattery and approval of others. We are free to be humble in Christ because we are completely at peace with him through his crucifixion and resurrection. We can rest even while we work because we are justified by faith, not works. We are free to serve God and others because we know that Christ will meet our needs out of the riches of his love. Pride is eliminated when we remember that "those who live should no longer live for themselves but for him who died for them and was raised again" (2 Cor. 5:15).

Detecting Pride

If humility involves knowing who we are as creatures of the Creator and as sinners rescued by the Redeemer, can humility be cultivated in such a way that Christ will be seen in us? Seeking humility is a delicate matter. We should guard against praying for humility in order to be seen as humble, for this is merely pride feigning humility for pride's sake. We can't pray for humility as we would pray for a pay raise at work. We must dig deeper because humility involves a fundamental adjustment of our inner being in accordance with the truths of the gospel. Let's consider several steps for detecting the pride that precludes humility.

First, we should beseech God to lay bare our offensive pride, as David did when he prayed, "Search me, O God, and know my heart; test me and know my anxious thoughts. See if there is any offensive way in me, and lead me in the way everlasting" (Ps. 139:23–24). We may need to turn our prayers from requests for material blessings to requests for the spiritual blessing of humility. This is eminently reasonable since nothing can truly be enjoyed without humility; pride is far too petty and protective to enjoy anything. Building the kingdom of self is a dirty and dispiriting business. Finding humility in the Spirit glorifies God and brings life and peace.

Second, we should note what things particularly disturb us and then ask, "Am I bothered because this is evil and offensive to God or am I upset because my pride is hurt?" Am I more outraged at not having my good deed applauded than I am over the fact that my friend was cheated by an employer? If so, my pride outweighs my humility. Murray puts it strongly: "All sharp and hasty judgments and utterances, so often excused under the plea of being outright and honest; all manifestations of temper and touchiness and irritation; all feelings of bitterness and estrangement— have their root in nothing but pride, that ever seeks itself."[4]

Third, whenever we promote ourselves, we fall into pride and make humility impossible. Everyone needs approval and encouragement, but no one should manipulate others in order to gain it. Boasting is a particular snare for those in public ministry where popular approval is so important. Instead of glorying in God's work through us and in us, a subtle shift occurs and we instead recite our deeds of righteousness in order to receive applause. But Proverbs says to "let another praise you, and not your own mouth; someone else, and not your own lips" (Prov. 27:2); it is not honorable to seek your own honor (Prov. 25:27). We disgrace God's ministry when we succumb to pride. But humility comes when our self-esteem is grounded in God's gracious estimation of us rather than in the varying opinions of others.

Seeking Humility

There are several ways that we can protect our hearts from pride and seek humility in the Spirit. First, in a culture enamored of self, we must be ever watchful not to let the world squeeze us into its psychological mold. The fountain of the spiritual life is humility, not self-love. In Christ we are free to recognize good qualities in ourselves and enjoy them as we offer them to God for his use, but exercises in self-congratulation are never edifying. As the spiritual advisor Fénelon put it, "True humility lies in seeing our own unworthiness and giving ourselves up to God, never doubting that He can work out the greatest results for and in us."[5] We are best suited for God's great purposes by realizing that he is great and we are not. This refutes the advice of a self-absorbed society that desperately seeks to inflate a sinful and unforgiven self to acceptable proportions. Paul put it best when he said, "We have this treasure in jars of clay to show that this all-surpassing power is from God and not from us" (2 Cor. 4:7).

Second, we can study and meditate upon the lives and writings of great saints and heroes of the faith, both within and outside of the Scripture, who put flesh and bone on humility. Here we find that humility is not the enemy of greatness. Moses was called the meekest of men, but he was a world-changing instrument in God's hands. Paul was a humble bondservant of Christ, but bold to preach the gospel and risk all for God. As someone involved with higher education, I find the example of Thomas Aquinas inspiring because I need to avoid the competitiveness and intellectual pride that besets academics. Aquinas was a great theologian and philosopher; yet one of his disciples wrote that he "owed his knowledge less to the effort of his mind than to the power of his prayer. Every time he wanted to study, discuss, teach, write, or dictate, he first had recourse to the privacy of prayer, weeping before God in order to discover the divine secrets." The great scholar was great only because he was humble. "Humility comes before honor" (Prov. 15:33).

Third, being open and accountable to another believer is essential to spiritual growth in humility. Humility is not a solitary project; it requires help from friends. My wife has on several occasions observed a sense of self-importance in my teaching and gently encouraged me to reform. I need to hear this even though it stings. The pain of correction is far better than the indulgence and deception of pride. Spouses and friends should prayerfully encourage each other to take up the yoke of Jesus in order to experience and express his restful humility.

Humility in the Public Square

Is the practice of Christian humility possible in the modern public square—the realm so often characterized by noisy, unprincipled, and power-mongering and power-brokering politicos who are more likely to believe that the earth inherits the meek than that the meek inherit the earth? In the power of Christ's spirit, and only in that power, is it possible . . . if rare. Furthermore, given what I have argued from Scripture, humility in the public realm is not merely possible but is a divine mandate for all Christian citizens because the ramifications of our salvation do not end where the public square begins. Christ is Lord over every aspect of reality and we must honor him with Christ-like character, as "far as the curse is found," as the great hymn puts it.

A sterling example of Christian humility wed to principled conviction was reported in the August 16, 1993, issue of *Christianity Today*. Responding to a piece of legislation in Philadelphia that would have granted the legal recognition of homosexual partners, Bill Devlin, director of the Philadelphia Christian Action Council, launched an effort to oppose the bill. Instead of condemning the opposition and mounting a campaign of ill will and shrill declarations (as has sadly been the case in similar culture wars around the country), Devlin led a multicultural and multi-ethnic coalition of Protestants, Catholics, and a Muslim cleric to successfully marshal what he called "a principled persuasion" to defeat the bill. Devlin rejected what he called the "Rambo Christian" approach in favor of calmly appealing to the best interests of the wider community without pridefully posturing as an ethical oracle in search of political muscle. May his numbers increase! The theme of demonstrating humility (or Christian civility) in the midst of the culture wars is carefully developed in Richard Mouw's excellent book, *Uncommon Decency* (Inter-Varsity, 1992).

Humility Is Not Optional

Humility is not optional for Christians. The humility of Jesus secured a salvation that makes humility both possible and necessary. It is not simply one virtue among many, but the root of all righteousness—because only humility puts us in our rightful place before the Creator and Redeemer. Empty vessels can be filled to overflowing with the Holy Spirit. Vessels brimming with pride can hold no grace. Pascal summarized the humble life when he said, "Do small things as if they were great, because of the majesty of Christ, who does them in us and lives our life, and great things as if they were small and easy, because of his almighty power."[6] Amen.

7

Apologetics, Truth, and Humility

Recently when I was discussing philosophy with an earnest undergraduate student, she informed me that she rejected the idea that she could know "*the* truth" because this would condemn everyone who disagreed with her. Since philosophers have traditionally exulted in winning arguments instead of eliminating them, I asked why she shunned victory in favor of terminal agnosticism. She explained, "If I claim to know the truth, then I must also claim that whoever disagrees with me is wrong, and that would make me intolerably arrogant." This student was suffering from a case of dislocated humility. Instead of being rightly humble about her ability always to know truly or infallibly, she was instead humble over the mere possibility of discovering the truth. She identified the idea of possessing truth with pride.

I suggested a shift in perspective: What if we view truth as something that might be discovered by diligent seekers? Then one who claims to know the truth need not be arrogant. She need not view herself pridefully as the owner or creator of truth, but could rather behave as a humble servant of truth who wants to make it known to others for their own good. She could thus humbly enter into dialogue over the matter by giving arguments and evidence to support her views.

The student reluctantly admitted that she had never thought of it that way before, and said she would think more about it. I prayed she would, because until she grasps the concept of attainable truth, she will never comprehend the identify of Christ, who is "the way and the truth and the life" (John 14:6).

This encounter highlights how crucial humility is to the Christian's apologetic task in a world steeped in relativism. On the one hand, we must place humility in the right place. We should never misplace our humility by disparaging the only thing that will ever set anyone free—the truth itself. The central claims of God's revelation should be understood, explained, and defended. I thank the one true God that those involved in apologetics ministries are providing sound reasons for the faith and are challenging the critics of Christianity.

On the other hand, ambitious Christian apologists often lose something indispensable in the process of defending the indispensable. In refusing to jettison the idea of truth, we often jettison humility instead. We can become, as the student feared, arrogant. We may hold the truth falsely.

It is dangerously easy for apologists to become prideful when we identify the truth with our ego instead of with God himself. Instead of contending for "the faith that was once for all entrusted to the saints" (Jude 3), we may end up contending for our own infallibility. We should heed Blaise Pascal, who wrote in his *Pensées* that "it is false piety to preserve peace at the expense of truth. It is also false zeal to preserve truth at the expense of charity." Several facts can point us toward the fruitful partnership of true piety and true zeal.

First, Christian truth is best defended when it is held both firmly and humbly—in the manner one would hold a newborn child. It is infinitely precious and therefore worth defending; but it is a gift not of our own making. We lay no claim to its greatness or even to the fact that we recognize it as truth (Eph. 2:8–9). We know by grace that grace may be known. If we speak of "our faith" we should emphasize that the truth is not our possession; rather the truth possesses us. No one put it better than G. K. Chesterton, who in *Orthodoxy* confessed concerning Christianity: "I will not call it my philosophy; for I did not make it. God and humanity made it; and it made me."

Second, our knowledge of biblical truth should grow over a lifetime. Biblical truth will always exceed my present understanding of biblical truth. The humble apologist will defend Christianity's core claims to the best of his ability—the inspiration of Scripture, the Trinity, the incarnation, justification by faith, and so on—while remaining open to discussion about less central and more debatable issues such as the particularities of eschatology or church government.

Third, Jesus said that the meek, not the belligerent, will inherit the earth. No matter how winsome the presentation, the gospel will offend those with hardened hearts; but we should avoid increasing the offense through arrogance. Paul is a model when he says, "We have this treasure in jars of clay to show that this all-surpassing power is from God and not from us" (2 Cor. 4:7). The principles of Paul's pastoral instruction to Timothy apply to all apologists: "And the Lord's servant must not quarrel; instead, he must be kind to everyone, able to teach, not resentful. Those who oppose him he must gently instruct, in the hope that God will grant them repentance leading them to a knowledge of the truth" (2 Tim. 2:24–25). Our aim should be to speak the truth in love (Eph. 4:15).

Fourth, no matter how adept our advocacy of the faith, we must glory in the Lord and not in our apologetic prowess. Without humility, even the best arguments will ring hollow. Our aim in defending the gospel is to set people free, not to defend ourselves or acquit ourselves of all error. The humble apologist stands valiantly for God's absolute, objective, and universal truth, even as he stands on feet of clay with an ear open to correction.

Fifth, whatever our skill at defending the faith, any humble presentation of Christian truth is a powerful tool in God's hands. The Lord opposes the proud and exalts the humble (Matt. 23:12; James 4:6). Christian humility is an arresting apologetic in and of itself. Those who with plain speech forget themselves in service of Christ outshine those who eloquently defend only their egos.

Let all apologists pray with Albert Outler: "Lord, protect us from the mindless love that deceives and the loveless truth that kills." Amen.

8

The Renewed Mind and Its Enemies

In C. S. Lewis's *Screwtape Letters,* the demon Screwtape writes to the junior demon Wormwood that "jargon, not argument, is the best ally" in keeping people from Christianity. Screwtape rejoiced that Wormwood's first target—a recent convert—was accustomed to having "a dozen incompatible philosophical ideas dancing about together inside his head" and that he seldom viewed ideas as "true" or "false" but rather in terms of their reputation as "academic," "practical," or "contemporary." The senior demon dreaded the possibility of Wormwood's charge engaging his intellect in matters Christian, for "the trouble with argument is that it moves the whole struggle onto the Enemy's own ground."

Demonic devaluation of reason and argument has ravaged our society. We wade eye-deep in reams of information, captives to our emerging "information society." We are buffeted by a bevy of facts and deluged by data—computer printouts, newspaper headlines, magazine stories, video screens—yet we often lack the ability to weigh the facts, to form sound judgments based on reasoned arguments. Rather than develop convictions, we sling opinions—often no better than superficial preferences—like pies in an old slapstick movie.

A powerful engine of this anti-intellectualism is television. Although we should give thanks for Christians who have successfully used the medium to advance the gospel without compromise, we should understand its limitations and liabilities. Television absorbs our senses—and increasingly so with big screens, stereo sound, and other technological wizardry—yet often disengages our minds.

We passively ingest visual impressions without intellectually digesting what is presented. We tend to believe the network that claims to be fit "to bring us the world"—in a half-hour news program, including commercials. We tend to believe that sitcoms are like "real life," and so impoverish our own. We tend to believe that watching a church service is the same as attending one (just use a stamped envelope instead of the collection plate). If we are not careful we will find ourselves in the devil's playground with television switched on and minds switched off.

Yet the apostle Paul urges us not to be conformed to this world—through television or anything else—but to be transformed through the renewing of our minds (Rom. 12:1–2). The renewed mind—a mind alive to the principles of Scripture by inspiration of the Holy Spirit—is the avowed enemy of jargon, superficial opinion, and irrationality. It searches for and utilizes truth; it exposes and corrects error. It develops its God-given rational powers in service of its Creator.

An intellectual antidote to the reigning irrationalism is the rediscovery of the discipline of reading, both of the Good Book and good books. Careful reading demands focused attention and so engages our intellect.

Television overwhelms us with a hurricane of visual images. A book lets us ponder what we read at our own pace (television can be watched at only one speed). Rather than being intoxicated by appearances, we may assess arguments. Rather than adopting superficial opinions we may develop reasoned convictions, and by doing so we will be poised to refute secular jargon masquerading as argument.

How do you respond to the secular slogans of our deluded day? What about the legitimacy of "doing your own thing," the innocence of "victimless crimes," the mandate to "separate church and state," the insistence that "you can't legislate morality"?

But which book, besides the Good Book? Sniff out some serious Christian readers and ask their advice. Don't be surprised if they faint with happiness and even offer to loan you their volumes! Also check the "Issues" and "Apologetics" section of your local Christian bookstore. These titles are usually not best-sellers, but this has little to do with their quality. Digesting the thoughts of modern Christian writers, such as C. S. Lewis, R. C. Sproul, and Francis Schaeffer, or classical authors such as Saint Augustine and Blaise Pascal can expand your intellectual horizons dramatically and thus frustrate the efforts of a hellish host of book-hating demons.

9

Information and Wisdom

Best-selling author John Naisbitt tells us that we are moving from the industrial age to the "information age"—the age of mass, relentless computerization. The rapidity of this change and the scope of its influence are overwhelming.

> While the shift from an agricultural to an industrial society took 100 years, the present restructuring from an industrial to an information society took only two decades. Change is occurring so rapidly that there is no time to react; instead we must anticipate the future.[1]

In the information age, the "knowledge theory of value" will dominate economics. Know-how (computer ingenuity) will replace labor in importance.

The information age results in an explosion of available information. We crave it, we love it; and our language reflects it. The word *informative* is thus a popular and complimentary adjective. People are respected if they are "knowledgeable." Jeremy Rifkin's stimulating book *Algeny* argues that modern society now views nature as a stockpile of genetic information awaiting our understanding and restructuring by genetic engineering. Biotechnologies become the new magic; the technical use of information becomes the new saving knowledge (*gnosis*).

While the information explosion provides tremendous opportunities for spreading the gospel and improving society in general, mere information is not necessarily valuable. Value consists not primarily in how much you know, but in how you use what you do know. R. J. Rushdoony hits home: "Learning alone is not enough, and learning alone can make a man simply a learned fool. And a learned fool is simply a more dangerous man than a simple, ignorant fool."[2]

Amassing facts or data is not the measure of godliness or of wisdom. Nevertheless, the data have become the new deity. Even before the information age, Richard Weaver clearly exposed this error. Speaking of "the astonishing vogue of factual information," he goes on to say:

> One notes that even in everyday speech the word *fact* has taken the place of *truth*; "it is fact" is now the formula for a categorical assertion. . . . The public is being taught systematically to make this fatal confusion of factual particulars with wisdom. On the radio and in magazines and newspapers appear countless games and quizzes designed to test one's stock of facts. The acquisition of unrelated details becomes an end in itself and takes the place of the true ideal of education.[3]

And when we consider the countless billions of bleary-eyed hours spent before the ubiquitous video game, we see that even facts are dispensed with—only visual images and manual dexterity remain.

An intellectual inflation is producing a new species, "homo up-to-datum," says historian Daniel J. Boorstin:

> Every hour of every day, information inflates our mental currency, stuffs our minds, and distracts us from thinking through the problems of our times. On TV and radio, in morning newspapers and computer readouts, flimsy "bits" of information inundate and confuse us. This flood of messages from the instant-everywhere fills every niche in our consciousness, crowding out knowledge and understanding.[4]

We stuff ourselves, he says, with the random and the miscellaneous. Yet God's wisdom confronts our condition. We are warned of those who are "always learning but never able to acknowledge the truth" (2 Tim. 3:7). Wisdom is to be sought from the hand of God, not in the ocean of miscellaneous facts. Wisdom, grounded in God's truth and built into personal lives, sorts out the facts and applies them toward the kingdom of God—a kingdom not merely of information, but of righteousness and truth. Our faith seeks understanding, not just facts. As Proverbs says: "Buy the truth and do not sell it; get wisdom, discipline and understanding" (23:23). Wisdom comes from God (James 1:5), not from mere information. And Wisdom calls out, understanding raises her voice: "You who are simple, gain prudence; you who are foolish, gain understanding" (Prov. 8:5).

God offers us wisdom in his Word and by his Spirit. It is wisdom that we and the world need. The age of information must be sanctified by the truly wise, lest the facts suffocate us. We must look to Christ, "the power of God and the wisdom of God" (1 Cor. 1:24). The truth of God's wisdom sets us free.

10

Putting Worship in the Worship Service

Worship is radically underrated in the church today. Its importance is routinely acknowledged in theory, but rarely in practice. I recently visited a large evangelical church that listed worship first in its fivefold statement of purpose. The Sunday morning I attended, the agenda was full. A video urged people to become involved in an outreach ministry of the church. There was a lengthy introduction, involving several speakers, of a newly organized system of fellowship groups for church members. Nine infants were dedicated. There was an offertory—a sentimental rendering of a sentimental song about personal Christian experience. There was, of course, the sermon. And, as has been the case in every evangelical church I have ever attended, the actual "worship" part of the "worship service" occupied the time that remained after all the important business had been scheduled. The time left over in this particular service allowed for one short hymn and one short praise song. Judging by the lackadaisical spirit with which the congregation sang these two songs, it is

Rebecca Merrill Groothuis wrote this chapter.

doubtful whether anyone noticed that the "worship" was missing from the "worship service."

Worship, in the sense of the corporate Christian celebration of God and our love relationship with him, is an activity pivotal to the spiritual health of both individual believers and the church. Why, then, is it so underrated? Perhaps because it seems, in this materialistic and pragmatic culture, to be pointless. What tangible purpose, after all, is accomplished when a group of people gather and sing together? Unless a church has an understanding of why we need to worship and what happens when we do worship, the "worship service" may provide instruction and fellowship, but it will not offer the God-centered, God-glorifying focus that comes from genuine worship.

What is worship, then, and why do we worship? Worship is both vocation and celebration. It is daily work done as unto the Lord for his glory; this is continual, living worship. Then there is also the conscious acting-out of this attitude in a kind of ritual celebration; this outward enactment of inward faith and conviction serves to strengthen that conviction. Although worship as celebration will be the focus of this chapter, it is important to remember that both ways of worship are interrelated and essential. The celebration grows out of the vocation, and the vocation is confirmed and further established by the celebration. Viewed rightly, our diverse vocations here on earth—the unique ways in which we each act out our devotion to God in service of his kingdom—are merely manifestations of our eternal vocation of worship.

The celebration of worship in the church service is both uniquely God-centered and uniquely people-centered. It is God-centered in that it is the one thing we do that is all to the glory of God. If at any point in worship we get the glory, it is no longer worship. Worship by its definition means to glorify God and enjoy him forever (in the wonderful words of the Westminster Catechism). Worship is a useless activity, this rejoicing and reveling in the glory and greatness of God. But it is wonderfully useless. For to the degree that worship is useless according to the pragmatically determined values of this present life, to that degree it is wonderfully purposive in the eternal order of things. Worship is at the heart of our eternal vocation as believers, because our love of God is at the heart of our worship. We worship God because we love him. And as we worship, God reveals himself and his love to us, thus freeing us to love and worship him more.[1]

Worship is also people-centered in that it is the one activity in the church in which, ideally, all the people participate. It leaves no one out and it favors no one over another; everyone is qualified, everyone is included. Indeed, if the people do not worship, it simply is not done. Worship is not a delegated task; the clergy cannot perform it on our behalf or for our benefit, as is the case with other ministries. Worship is the people's ministry.

This is one of the wonderful things about worship: we all can always participate. There are no qualifications in terms of talent or training, race, class, or sex. Anyone—no matter her gifts, accomplishments, or station in life—can worship as well as anyone else. One need only be a believer who loves the Lord. But worship is no fringe activity, the work left over for those unable to pursue the more important occupations. Worship of God is the chief vocation for which we all were created. This is the one thing that will make our lives worthwhile, and without which any life, no matter how exemplary or impressive, is ultimately worthless.

This puts everything into perspective. No matter how many of my efforts in this life fail, if I remain a worshiper I will not have failed at the most important thing. The only way I can fail at worship is simply to refuse to do it. And the only way I can fail in my Christian life is simply to refuse to worship. God's demands and standards are so different from our own. He is unimpressed by our wealth, fame, and achievements. He simply wants our worship. Certainly, we should be obedient and faithful in doing the other things in life that need doing. But those are not the things by which we identify, authenticate, and vindicate ourselves in God's eyes. Our "success" as persons rests on nothing but our willingness—yea, eagerness—to glorify God and enjoy him forever.

Worship is not only our most important vocation, but also the most enduring. Of all that we do in this life, worship alone will remain in the next. Worship of God is the organizing principle, the chief occupation, of the citizens in heaven. So it ought to be for believers on earth. Most of the skills we must learn in order to get along successfully in this life will be of no use in heaven: treating the physically ill, producing and consuming numerous goods and services helpful in protecting us from a hostile and hazardous environment, litigating and mediating between parties full of hostility toward one another, carefully protecting the egos of those in power over us, and so forth. Even the work of the "ministry"—such as evangelizing the unsaved, counseling the emotionally devastated, providing services for the socially disadvantaged—will be unnecessary in heaven. But when we invest ourselves in learning to worship, we are making an investment in a skill that will be essential throughout eternity.

The relationship between worship and work—or worship as celebration and worship as vocation—is summed up beautifully by Ben Patterson:

> There is a wonderful and pregnant ambiguity in the Bible's words for work and worship: in both the Old and New Testaments the word for each is the same. . . . Only the context determines which meaning should be selected by the translator. . . . In the Bible there is an indissoluble unity between worship and work, since both are forms of service to God. There is the service we render to God in our worship and there is the service we render to him in our work. The former is the liturgy of the sanctuary, the latter is the liturgy of the world. But of the two forms of work—or worship, if you will— it is only the liturgy of the sanctuary that is eternal. Whatever you happen to be doing now from nine to five will one day pass away. . . . Even the work we do for the kingdom of God will outlive its usefulness. . . . But the work of worship will go on forever.[2]

Knowing God

Worship requires not only that we love God but also that we know him. The Bible says we are to worship God in spirit and in truth (John 4:23). We know the truth about God by measuring our understanding of who he is with what the Bible says about him. Worship is not a purely mystical activity; mental effort is required as well.

How we live is determined by how and whom we worship, which in turn is determined by how we see God—by who we understand him to be. Knowledge of God does not come simply by a supranatural visitation of the Holy Spirit that bypasses our minds and touches only our hearts. Knowing God is a matter for the whole person, and the mind serves a vital purpose in preparing our hearts for worship and in safeguarding our worship from idolatry. We must, in short, have at least a rudimentary knowledge of theology. The more we know about God, the more moved we will be to worship him. (One of the most remarkable times of worship I ever had took place in a theology class. In the midst of a discussion of the attributes of God, we were unexpectedly and powerfully overwhelmed by the wonder of such a God, and discussion dissolved into worship.)

As we align our understanding of God with the biblical doctrine of God's nature and attributes, we are also protected from the idolatry of fashioning a god from our own imaginations. It is all too easy, especially in churches that emphasize personal experience, for our worship of God to degenerate into an idolizing of our mental state during the "worship experience." When a person constructs a god out of his own imagination, his god is his imagination, and he is guilty of self-worship, which is idolatry. The worshiping Christian must remember that God is an objective reality, not a subjective mental state. God exists independently of anyone's imagination, and to worship him necessarily requires that one turn one's attention away from contemplation of his own subjective experience and toward the God who is objectively "there."

But this business of knowing God truly is not the strenuous task it might seem to be, because it is God's earnest desire to make himself known to us. Throughout the Bible, especially in the Old Testament prophetic books, it seems that all God really wants is our recognition and acknowledgment of who he is. God's great desire is to reveal himself to us so that we may see him as he is. Once we see him thus, everything else follows: the worship, the repentance, the obedience. We ought to understand God's desire to be known and loved, because we have it too. It is a part of what it means to be personal and social beings, like the one in whose image we were made. One of the strongest drives we have is to be known, to demonstrate to others who we are, what we are like, what we know, and what we can do—and, we hope, to be loved for it. Likewise, one of the deepest and longest-lasting emotional pains any of us experience is the pain of being misunderstood and rejected by those who do not bother to get to know us. We would gladly have shared ourselves—but they would not. Surely we can appreciate God's strong desire for us to know him and to respond to his revelation of himself in openness, worship, and trust.[3]

Not only is our worship grounded in our knowledge of God, it is also a means by which we grow in our knowledge of the Lord. We love and worship God because he has revealed himself to us in love; and as we worship him, our spirits are opened to receive a further revelation of who God is and how he loves us. This increased knowledge of God increases our desire to worship him. In giving ourselves to worship that is pure and true, we offer ourselves unconditionally to God; he in turn sanctifies us further, freeing us from ourselves so that our worship can become even more pure and true. George MacDonald says it well: "It is the nature of God, so terribly pure that it destroys all that is not pure as fire, which demands like purity in our worship. He will have purity. It is not that the fire will burn us if we do not worship thus; . . . [but that it] will go on burning within us after all that is foreign to it has yielded to its force, no longer with pain and consuming, but as the highest consciousness of life, the presence of God."[4]

This aspect of worship, which is God's response to us, is often missed in a culture that focuses on self-expression: worship is perceived merely as an expression of our feelings about God— usually concerning what he can do for us rather than who he is in himself. The other side—that of God making himself known to us—goes unacknowledged. As a result, our worship songs tend to be simplistic and self-centered, adequate perhaps for an expression of our own feelings, but woefully deficient as a means by which the glory and greatness of God can be revealed to us. We not only misunderstand the nature and purpose of worship, we miss the importance of the quality of the music that we employ in our service of worship. It matters what kind of music we use in worship. The more glorious the music, the greater its capacity to reveal the glory of God.

Worshiping as "Artists"

Music is an utterance, a communication, a message. This is the nature of any kind of art. It is the word or voice of the artist expressed in tangible form. The urge to create is prompted in the human heart by the fact that God created humans in his image. It is part of our commission as human beings to be creative and expressive, true to the One in whose likeness we are made. Being made in the image of God means that we were made to be a reflection of his glory. If human art were perfect, and the reflection it gave were wholly clear and unclouded by human sin, then we should see in it not only our own image, but the reflection of the Lord God himself, in whose image we were made.

God's desire is to redeem the art of his people, that it might clearly reflect his glory and speak forth his praise. A Christian need not be a Beethoven or a Michelangelo to create under divine inspiration. God's purpose is to speak through his people. His was, in effect, a double-barrelled creative effort: God created creators to create for him. Thus, our works are actually to be his works, our words his words. We are to become a channel through which God's own glory and creativity may flow.

There is a vital relationship between worship and art. Both involve communication—the outward expression of an inward state of being. In worship, a person gives all that she is and has to the Lord. True worship is continual; it does not begin and end with the church service. But it is during the worship service that the worshiping attitude of daily life is formally expressed in a public act. The singing and other activities that take place in the church service are a ritualized expression of what is to every true believer a way of life. Singing the praises of God is outward confirmation in a symbolic act of what should be to the soul a continual inner reality. As our relationship with God is thus celebrated and acted out, it is established in our thoughts and our lives. This is the function of any kind of art; it serves as a kind of celebration or sacrament of life. Art reminds us to keep on living, and in its act of confirming existence, makes it all worthwhile.

If worship is an art, then worshipers are artists, expressing in tangible form the attitude of their hearts toward God—embodying the spirit of praise. As worshiper/artists, we reveal something of God's own glory and creativity. Our songs of praise express the very word of God that dwells within us—thereby ensuring that God is praised as he is worthy of being praised. For the Lord has graciously seen fit to use us as vessels to fill, as instruments to play upon, in bringing glory to his name.

Worship music should be both of and unto the Lord. It is to be of the Lord in the sense that the message of our music is to be the word of the Lord in us being expressed through us. Music that is saturated with the Spirit of God will truly be worship "in spirit and in truth," for it will be the Spirit of God expressing the truth of his word through the music we offer him.

Worship music is also to be unto the Lord, in that our first ministry as Christians is always to God in worship. Unless the focus is on ministering to God in worship, a church service becomes a performance in which those on the platform play their respective roles and those in the pews passively assess the situation. But a worship service is not meant to be an act the ministers stage before the people; it is to be an act the people stage before God. He is the audience and all that we do is to be unto him. This is our ministry to the Lord, our reasonable service of worship—the conscious, intelligent act of presenting ourselves as a living sacrifice unto God. The criterion of good worship music is not how well it blesses us, but how well it blesses the Lord; our goal should be to please and honor him. Praise songs that are simplistic and self-serving do not accomplish this purpose.

When music of artistic integrity is anointed by the Lord and offered to the Lord, the music serves a purpose greater than being an aid to worship that helps people "get into" the "worship experience." Such music serves not only as an expression of our love for God, but also as a revelation of God's glory. It is not only our offering to God; in a much higher sense, it is his gift to us. Through worship music, God can make himself known to us more fully.

And worship will follow revelation, instantly and spontaneously. To see the Lord is to worship him. Ideally, worship music that is offered to the Lord will be so expressive of and filled with his Spirit, his power, and his praise, that people cannot but fall at his feet and worship him.

This, then, is the central purpose of the worship service—to connect the people with God, to usher in the presence of the Holy One. It is with pleasure that the Lord receives us into his presence, pouring himself into us as we pour ourselves out before him, responding to his presence with sacrifices of praise and adoration.

It is from this view of worship that we see most clearly the end to which we were saved: it was not primarily for our blessing and happiness (although there certainly are benefits to salvation), but rather to bring glory to God. When we come to church to worship, we come to desire and enjoy God for who he is, rather than for what we can receive from him. Although true worship offered from a pure heart yields pleasure in the presence of the Lord, the worship service should be seen as fundamentally God-serving rather than self-serving. We come first to bless the Lord, and secondarily to be blessed by him.

Choosing Musical Styles in Worship

There are two components of a worship service: substance and style. The substance of worship is the attitude of the worshipers; the style is the form in which that attitude is expressed. Worship can be and is expressed in a wide variety of styles. But there is a sense in which the substance of the worship is constrained by its formal expression.

The worship style adopted by a particular church is largely a product of that church's view of culture in general and art in particular. A church that is uninterested in culture and views art as a means to an instrumental end will assume a worship style that is simple (often simplistic) and easily accessible to people with relatively little education or interest in the finer things of culture. Such a style of worship lends itself to expression only of emotion and not of thoughtful content. A simple worship style with popular appeal is usually well suited to evangelistic services in that it meets the people where they are.

When a church pays little or no attention to developing a theology of culture, then it will take the path of least resistance. Such a church will either follow the lead of popular culture or react against it by developing its own subculture that is nonetheless on the same level of appeal to "the common man."

It is no coincidence that those churches that most readily incorporate elements of contemporary culture into their worship services are also least likely to appreciate the need to confront and to transform contemporary culture according to biblical truth. It is likewise the case that those churches whose worship is most rigidly removed from current styles are least likely to perceive that there are elements in "secular" culture that are compatible with biblical truth and therefore worth conserving.

The worship style of a church both affects and is affected by that church's view of culture. The medium often serves as the message, and those in the pews may draw conclusions about the relationship of the church to the world, based on how the style of worship music compares to the music of the outside culture. Therefore, selecting the type of music used in worship is not a trivial concern, but one with deep theological significance. It not only determines the parameters of the quality of worship, but also ramifies in areas other than the worship service, such as how church members may come to weigh being "in the world" against being "of the world."

A church that has an interest in cultural and artistic endeavors will have a concern to develop a style of worship that is characterized by artistic integrity. This lends itself to a formal expression of worship that is rich and deep enough to encompass thoughtful reflection concerning the nature of the God we worship, as well as an emotional response of praise and thanksgiving to such a great God. A worship style that conserves the best in secular culture past and present, and employs it in the service of God—thus transforming it for his glory—does not merely meet the people where they are. Rather, such worship lifts them up and urges them on toward a fuller understanding of God and a richer expression of worship.

But a worship style that devalues culture and fails to heed the call to artistic excellence and integrity acts as a brake on worship itself. When the style of worship stops short of the full intellectual and aesthetic potential of the worshipers, then the worship falls short of the creative and excellent offering of praise and adoration that our Lord deserves to receive from his people.

Of course, the greatest art in the world is not worthy of God. Yet how much more are we able to comprehend and respond in worship to the greatness of God when we have developed fully our God-given abilities in creative and artistic expression? And in receiving such an offering, how can God not be pleased?

Encouraging artistic integrity in worship does not mean that the nonmusicians in the church are unqualified to worship and minister to the Lord in music. It is possible for music to be technically simple, yet still be true art capable of expressing the Spirit of God and the worshipers' love for God. Ministers of music should try to enlarge the people's artistic capacities by leading them in songs of "simple art" and teaching ways in which they can creatively minister to the Lord. Every worshiper is an artist in his own right, and when he offers the best that he can give, it is a ministry acceptable and pleasing unto the Lord. God does not care how much we give, but whether or not we keep back anything for ourselves. He uses best those worshipers who are wholly his, that he may create through them a song of praise that is wholly his.

But cultural refinement and discernment in worship style does not in itself guarantee a high quality of worship. The substance of worship, aside from its stylistic limitations of expression, depends on the people's understanding of the purpose of going to church. If the worship service is seen primarily as a time for the people to be entertained and/or uplifted, there will be little substance to the worship. But if the people gather together in order to glorify God, enjoy his presence, and come to know and serve him better, then their worship will be true, deep, and substantial. A worshipful attitude, however, does not come naturally to people. Both the substance and the style of worship must be carefully cultivated if worship is to be a true celebration of who God truly is.

Becoming Cultured and Christian

But what about the age-old worry that if the medium of worship (usually music) becomes so aesthetically exalted, the worshiper will worship the music rather than the God of whom the music speaks? The concern is a legitimate one, but it has had the unfortunate effect of convincing most Christians that spiritual maturity entails cultural mediocrity. A hunger for the things of God is assumed to rule out a desire for the finer things of culture (i.e., that which engages and develops the aesthetic and intellectual aspects of a person). After all, doesn't the Bible say something about "not many . . . wise, not many . . . noble" (1 Cor. 1:26)?

But there is no commandment in the Bible that enjoins believers to avoid wisdom or nobility. The point rather is that the wise and the noble will be more strongly tempted to pride and therefore more likely to succumb to pride and less likely to bow in repentance and worship before the Lord. The evil here is not wisdom and nobility, but pride. For that matter, it is possible for the uncultured and uneducated Christian to take pride in his "humility." And if art is a vessel, the capacity of which increases with its degree of excellence, then how can we deny our worship of our matchless God its fullest and finest expression? How can we settle smugly into a monolithic mediocrity?

There is an answer to this problem. Whether our worship consists of participating in the pews or performing on the platform, if our hearts are focused on the God of whom we sing or speak rather than on the form of our singing and speaking, then we can be as excellent as we are able and our worship will redound only to God's glory. In fact, under such conditions, the finer the expression of worship, the more fully God will be glorified—because he will be more fully revealed.

The more perfect the music, or, for that matter, the more profound and even poetic the preaching, the more our spiritual insight is sharpened to perceive the beauty, the wisdom, and the greatness of God. A fine expression of worship from a pure heart should inspire a larger vision of God and, in turn, a deeper and truer worship of him. In other words, the vessel is never too large if it is used to pour out praise that is potent and pure and free of pride.

Those Christians who are skilled musicians have a special responsibility to offer unto the Lord the best of their musical talents. If they fail to put their art to the service of the Lord in worship, whether out of laziness or a misguided sense of humility, they withhold from God the glory that is due him. But the creation and performance of artistically profound musical works must be prompted only by a desire to give utterance to a love for God that is itself so profound that it can find no other adequate means of expression. Great music not only is capable of great anointing, but also demands it. A surface sprinkling of God's blessing on an essentially human effort will not do. The message must always be at least equal to the medium. When the music is itself of great stature, there must be a corresponding spiritual stature in its message, motivation, and performance.

What would happen if churches began focusing on ministry to God in worship before they concentrated on ministry to others? If "upreach" preceded outreach? If church growth were seen as a product of the spiritual growth of its members? If, as a result, there was such a desire to offer mighty praises to God that only the best music came to be seen as an appropriate expression of such worship? Spiritual revival, effective evangelism, artistic and intellectual integrity, cultural influence without compromise, yes, and even church growth would doubtless follow such a revolution in the perception of the place and purpose of the worship service.

Let us, therefore, take seriously the task of perfecting the art of worship. This is not only a duty; it is a delight. For in worship more than in any other activity we begin to realize the meaning of our existence, and the reality of God's.

Part Three

Culture on Trial

11

Christianity
Lifestyle or Salvation?

Blaise Pascal, seventeenth-century philosopher, scientist, and Christian, aptly observed that "truth is so obscure in these times, and falsehood so established, that, unless we love the truth, we cannot know it." Twentieth-century society is not the first to turn its back on the question, What is true? But our society seems to have gone a step further than this. Not only the question of truth is neglected, but the very concept of truth seems to have been abandoned. "Religion" has been reduced to a mere mood, a choice, or a lifestyle. Truth is no longer an issue.

How many times have we heard Christianity referred to as if it were just one option among many equally legitimate "religious preferences"? "Christianity may be true for you," people say, "but it isn't true for me." The "truth" of a belief has come to be verified solely by its emotional function; reasonable reflection on religious doctrine is considered irrelevant. Religious belief is not compelled because it pertains to actual, objective truth, but chosen because it is somehow useful. Faith is considered true only

This chapter was written with Rebecca Merrill Groothuis.

87

to the extent that it produces desirable results (such as a good self-image).

True to this modern emphasis, Jesus is often marketed as a means to self-fulfillment. In our world of "overchoice" (Toffler) and self-centered ideals, people are concerned to choose their lifestyle, not to find their salvation—to escape failure, not hell; to attain assurance of success, not of heaven.

But biblical Christianity stands in direct opposition to this maladjusted mindset. Throughout Scripture, God reveals himself as the one God who towers above all. "Apart from me there is no God" (Isa. 44:6), he declares. God jealously guarded his people Israel and commanded their exclusive worship. Idolatry was not considered an acceptable "alternative lifestyle"; it often carried with it fatal consequences. Scripture repeatedly speaks of God as a rock (2 Sam. 22:32; Ps. 62:2)—an apt metaphor for the unchanging objective reality of his existence and the unavoidable implications of his word and rule for us. If we obey, that rock will be for us a shelter and protection; if we rebel, we will stumble over that rock and fall (1 Pet. 2:6–8).

There can be no getting around the God of the Bible (Ps. 139). He stubbornly exists as he is. "The earth is the LORD's and everything in it; the world, and all who live in it" (Ps. 24:1). We are his property, like it or not!

Jesus himself declared that he was the only way, truth, and life (John 14:6). Because of this, every area of life is under Christ's lordship. Biblical Christianity is nothing less than a total world view, an all-encompassing life purpose and perspective. The truth of Christianity has serious and far-reaching implications—not just in the individual Christian's personal, emotional experience, but in the society at large. Christ is bigger than our feelings.

But the truth claims of Christianity are nothing if not obnoxious and even outrageous to the modern mentality. After all, isn't tolerance and open-mindedness the name of the game today? "Live and let live"—no matter what lifestyle is chosen? It is not the accepted thing for one "religious preference" to single itself out from many other "religious preferences" and insist on restoring and restructuring every sphere of life according to its own standards. Nor is it acceptable for one lifestyle unequivocally to resist compromise with rival lifestyles. But this is Christianity writ large over the face of modern pluralism. A vigorously biblical Christianity must be both comprehensive and exclusive.

Christianity has not always been at loggerheads with Western culture. Several hundred years ago Christianity was the culturally accepted world view in the Western world. But through the intellectual compromises of the Renaissance (fourteenth to sixteenth centuries) and the Enlightenment (eighteenth century), the philosophical seeds were planted for naturalism, a world view that assumes everything is only matter in motion and ultimately lacking purpose or meaning. Things may evolve, but for no real end. Naturalism—also variously called secular humanism and materialism—gradually displaced Christianity as the sanctioned world view of elite society, shaping cultural institutions so that now in the twentieth century textbooks assume it, professors teach it, newspapers print it, and television networks broadcast it. We do fine without such totalitarian ideas as one God over all.

Because naturalism recognizes only the material world as real and ignores the spiritual, it consigns all religious "options" to the realm of helpful or harmful illusions. Naturalism is antisupernatural, so it will not take seriously Christianity's claim to truths such as the existence of God and the soul, angels and demons, heaven and hell. From a naturalistic standpoint, religion is judged solely according to its social usefulness. Naturalism decrees that no supernatural religion can be true in the usual sense of truth—that of corresponding to objective reality. Rather, religious "truth" is redefined to designate various ways in which various people can gain a sense of inner, subjective satisfaction. Naturalism is purely secular; it therefore privatizes and trivializes the sacred.

Despite naturalism's dim view of religion, people persist in their attempts to reach transcendence, to escape the stifling confines of a material and ultimately meaningless universe. Humans hunger for things supernatural; but concerning such things naturalism offers nothing beyond skepticism. So the marketplace of religious ideas is a potpourri of personal preferences chosen on the basis of their pragmatic value in the private lives of those who "believe." Such is the status of the burgeoning New Age movement in our culture. It is a religious belief system which itself defies naturalism, but is accommodated by society's naturalistic norms as just another religious option that "works" for some people but not all people. Religious pluralism (the diversity of religious options) in our culture is compatible with and is nourished by the overall framework of naturalistic assumptions.

Sociologist Peter Berger characterizes the modern situation "as a near-inconceivable expansion of the areas of human life open to choices." Things that once were accepted as cultural "givens"—sexual norms, vocational opportunities, religious beliefs, for example—have now become matters of personal choice. The fact that some of these traditional "givens" (such as those restricting vocational opportunity) deserve to be discarded while others (such as those restricting sexual behavior) ought to be retained serves only to compound the social confusion of overchoice.

The confusion is especially critical in the area of religious belief. Because, as Berger observes, individuals need a "plausibility structure" (social confirmation and consensus) to maintain their beliefs, people today are overwhelmed by ambivalence concerning religion. Modern society does not provide the necessary sociological support for Christianity, so for many people Christian beliefs are no longer considered plausible or compelling in any final sense; rather, they are optional. Life is a multiple-choice test in which any religious answer is permitted and none is required.

Pluralism thus has both a legal and a psychological effect. A pluralistic society provides legally for the free exercise of any religion—provided, of course, that such free exercise does not transgress other civil laws. But the psychological effect of a pluralistic society with a plethora of religious options is to regard them all as optional, alternative lifestyles. When this happens, religious belief is no longer viewed as staking a claim on objective reality—that which is stubbornly there whether or not anyone believes it—but rather is viewed as a matter of psychology. Religion is privatized, relegated to the personal, church-going, devotional life of the believer; for that is the only place where religious belief is allowed to exist with any validity. When Christianity is squeezed into this narrow, irrelevant mold, it becomes something other than the vibrant, compelling faith of the Bible.

Society becomes secularized when the plausibility of the religious world view is weakened and its applicability narrowed. Different areas of life are compartmentalized into the sacred (individual, personal life) and the secular (institutional, public life). Once religion is banished to the "sacred" sphere, it "cannot any longer fulfill the classical task of religion, that of constructing a common world within which all of social life receives ultimate meaning binding on everybody" (Berger). The more the "secular" is relegated to the secularists, the narrower becomes the scope and impact of the sacred. Christians who shun political issues, for example, may find that they cannot legally give their children a genuinely Christian education because of excessive state regulations. The secular stands at the door and knocks—or rips off the hinges when necessary.

As the secular impinges on it, the sacred itself becomes secularized. The church is worldly to the extent that it allows the world to dictate its cultural expression, whether this is reflected in an attempt to retreat from the world entirely (as in extreme fundamentalism) or to join up with the world (as in theological liberalism). Usually, in fact, the religious retreat of the conservative Christian from the secular world results only in the adoption of cultural values taken from the secular society of an earlier era. Many Christians, it seems, have lost the ability to apply biblical principles with integrity and transforming power to the whole of life and culture.

Religion becomes "subjectivized" in a society that is secularized. Because a naturalistic and pluralistic orientation provides no objective answers to the basic questions of life, moderns are obliged to look within to construct whatever certainties they can. But according to the Christian world view, truth is determined not by subjective preference but by objective reference to God's revelation in Scripture.

While Christian truth is not subjectively determined, it is subjectively received "by faith"—a faith based on fact, not fancy. As Christian philosopher Arthur Holmes put it, "I can passionately believe in a certain objective reality without violating either my intellectual integrity or the universality of truth."

Christianity is objectively true and subjectively compelling. We need not—indeed, we dare not—allow modernity to pare it down to such dimensions as are acceptable in the secular society. The claims of Christianity are exclusive, and their implications are comprehensive. To put the message of the Bible into one of the privatized "religion boxes" prepared by pluralism is to treat the Bible falsely. The Christ of true Christianity will not be so confined. He is Lord of all creation; there is no area of life exempt from his world and rule. We who are his are called to serve him as he is, and to resist the tendency to make him serve us as the self-help god our pluralized, secularized society would have him to be.

Christianity offers the world salvation on God's terms, not just another self-styled lifestyle.

12

Confronting the Challenge of Ethical Relativism

An indispensable pillar of Christian truth is the proposition that God is the lawgiver and moral governor of the universe. God is a personal and moral being, unlike the impersonal and amoral Force of New Age imagination. What is good, right, and virtuous is grounded in the triune God of the Bible. Jesus said, "Be perfect, therefore, as your heavenly Father is perfect" (Matt. 5:48).

Because the all-knowing and eternal God is the source and standard of ethics, the moral law is universal, absolute, and objective; it is based on his unchanging, holy character. Although the application of unchanging moral principles may change throughout history, the principles themselves are perpetually binding and irrevocable. God isn't morally moody.

Given this eternal anchorage for ethics, sin must be seen as the transgression of God's law. John says that "sin is lawlessness" (1 John 3:4). David cries out to God and says, "Against you, you only, have I sinned and done what is evil in your sight" (Ps. 51:4). Sin is an offense against God, ourselves, and others. R. C. Sproul calls it "cosmic treason"; we rebel against our creator.

In the modern Western world, ethical relativism poses a challenge to the biblical basis for ethics. Relativism affirms that moral right and wrong are only socially and individually determined. Ethics is split off from any objective moral order. Cultural norms of morality are relative to particular societies, individuals, and historical periods. What is "right for you" may not be "right for me." What is wrong today may not be wrong tomorrow. When the idea of moral law is held in disrespect, the notion of sin softens and then dissolves. If all is relative, absolute evil is impossible. If sin is nonsense, then the notion of a Savior from sin is absurd. There is nothing from which to be saved.

Because it denies abiding ethical standards and sin against a holy God, relativism is a roadblock to effective evangelism—besides undercutting values essential for a healthy society. But the key arguments for relativism are fatally flawed.

Relativists often argue that a society that honors free speech and freedom of religion must relinquish any notion of absolute truth or morality because this stifles the free exchange of ideas. Dogmatism and moralism are unwelcome in the pluralistic public square. Relativism is seen as required for a democracy of ideas and norms.

But this is flatly false. One may believe there are moral absolutes and also believe that the best way to reach ethical conclusions is through open discussion, dialogue, and debate. Freedom of religion and speech does not necessitate that there can be no objectively true religion or morality. A free society guarantees your right to be right—and your right to be wrong! I can try to persuade you of the truth of my convictions without using coercion. In fact, I may take it as a moral absolute that I should not coerce those I believe to be absolutely wrong.

The relativist has abandoned the concept of objective moral truth. It is all a matter of opinion because everything is relative. There is, therefore, nothing objective to argue about and no good reason to believe one thing over another. This is hardly what the American founders envisioned for a free society. It more resembles anarchism and nihilism (i.e., rejection of all values) than a "marketplace of ideas."

The sheer diversity of moral and religious ideas within and between societies is invoked as evidence for relativism. With so many options before us, who is to say what is true or false, right or wrong? We are left with relativism.

Here again, the facts do not deliver the conclusion. A diversity of ethical and religious beliefs hardly insures that they are all somehow true. A tribal culture may be scientifically wrong in thinking that the sun revolves around a flat earth. Why can't the same culture be ethically wrong for practicing head-hunting? If you say that abortion is right and I say it is wrong, how can we both be correct when we contradict each other? Ethical relativism eliminates the notion of a moral mistake. But this is just as fallacious as saying that every answer on a multiple-choice test is correct because there is a diversity of answers.

There may also be less diversity between cultures than is often thought. Every culture has taboos against stealing. Yet a desert culture may penalize the theft of water much more severely than would a tropical culture. The diversity of moral codes does not rule out a basic agreement on deeper ethical principles. In an appendix to his excellent book against relativism, *The Abolition of Man,* C. S. Lewis listed common moral principles spanning thousands of years from diverse religions and civilizations. As Paul tells us in Romans 1–2, God has endowed with a conscience all those created in his own image, however much we efface or neglect it.

Relativism also leads to absurd conclusions that undermine its credibility. If there is no true moral law that applies transculturally, then there is no basis for one culture to condemn actions in another. Surely any morally sane person must ethically condemn Nazi atrocities as evil and praise the heroes who resisted the Reich by saving Jews from extermination. But relativism cannot permit such judgments. The morality of everything is relative—even genocide.

If we can reveal flaws in the case for relativism, we can further argue that the moral law is best understood as flowing from the moral lawgiver of the universe. God, as our Creator, knows what is best for us and calls us to obey him for our own good and for his glory. Yet, as Paul said, "all have sinned and fall short of the glory of God" (Rom. 3:23). The universal fact of guilt and shame testifies to that, whatever the cultural setting might be.

But the good news is that the Lawgiver is also the Redeemer of those who lament over their lawlessness and trust in Jesus Christ as their Savior. Those who cry out, "God, have mercy on me, a sinner" (Luke 18:13), can find mercy and eternal life. But the unrepentant relativist must face the absolute justice of a holy God who admits no interpretation other than his own. In the end everything *is* relative—but it is relative to God's absolute standards, not ours.

13

The Smorgasbord Mentality

B ut Christ is true for you," the graduate student fumed. "If you believe it, then it's true *for you.*"

"No! Please let me explain," I insisted as a few onlookers gathered in the student union. "I'm saying that Christianity is true, *and* I believe it. It's not true *because* I believe it. It's true whether anyone believes it or not. At least understand what it claims!"

"Look," he sneered, "if it's true for you, fine; but it's not true for me. Get it!?"

I got it, but he did not. Faith for this typical modern was mere arbitrary belief. Truth—or what was left of it—had as many faces as there are people. He was a victim of pluralism.

We often hear that we live in a pluralistic society. This phrase gets much mileage without much understanding. We may think it means freedom of speech or religious liberty: In America, unlike many countries, everyone is free to express a viewpoint. It is also sometimes used to mean we should not pass judgment on others or that we should keep our opinions to ourselves. But is that pluralism? And how does it affect our culture and the way people view the gospel? How can we effectively communicate Christ in a pluralistic age?

Pluralism refers to a diversity of religions, world views, and ideologies existing at one time in the same society. We are socially heterogeneous. One religion or philosophy doesn't command and control the culture. Instead, many viewpoints coexist. We have Buddhists and Baptists, Mormons and Methodists, Christian Reformed and Christian Scientist—all on the same block, or at least in the same city. This can have a leveling effect on religious faith. The sheer number of religious options—check the Yellow Pages under "Churches"—tends to blunt the distinctiveness and credibility of any one of the many options. Simply put, if there are so many beliefs to choose from, how can we know which one is right? In light of this dizzying diversity we tend to make religious belief a personal, private choice, rather than a claim to objective truth. So we use words like "religious preference" and "lifestyle" to describe our personal choices, ethics, world views, and religious faith.

Whereas pluralism once meant religious liberty and political diversity, it is now often used to mean a philosophical relativism in which no one "religious preference" is allowed to stand in judgment of others. Each is seen as simply one entrée in the social smorgasbord, and all are equally acceptable. To assert or argue otherwise is to be "closed-minded"—the mortal sin against modern pluralism.

Christians should applaud our nation's traditional defense of religious liberty and freedom of speech. We have fought for it and we want to live by it. In this sense, we can say a hearty "Amen" to pluralism. But another pluralism is perversely polluting our thinking as a culture, and logic is one of its first victims. Vagueness, imprecision, and even stupidity surround the notion that religions, world views, or ideologies are "true" and legitimate because they all exist in the same culture. It is a sure sign of intellectual laziness (or suicide) to assert that any belief is "true" for anyone who believes it. Mutually contradictory beliefs cannot logically both be true. We may live next door to a nice Mormon family yet must say that both Christianity and Mormonism cannot be true.

But in the pluralistic situation, religious certainty ("Here I stand," as Martin Luther said) and well-thought-out convictions are often replaced by a noncommittal tentativeness. "Open-mindedness" and "tolerance" become the virtues. Philosopher-novelist Ayn Rand saw our modern open-mindedness as "a call for perpetual skepticism, for holding no firm convictions and granting plausibility to anything."[1]

Granting plausibility to anything also means granting certainty to nothing. The spirit of relativistic pluralism indicts certainty and firm conviction as closed-minded. Being closed-minded is to be closed to the plurality of options. How rude! How exclusivistic! But these accusations mean nothing if what we firmly believe is indeed objectively true. Granted that one may be certain of an untruth; but certainty itself is not to be shunned. Misplaced certainty—deception—is error; but certainty should be the passionate goal of every active mind. A certain mind must be closed to some things because if filters out truth from error. It must—to use an unpopular word—discriminate. Rand amplifies this by saying, "An active mind does not grant equal status to truth and falsehood; it does not remain floating in a stagnant vacuum of uncertainty; by assuming the responsibility of judgment, it reaches firm convictions and holds them."[2]

Christianity is anchored in the firm, certain conviction that Jesus Christ is "the way and the truth and the life." Christ is the God-man, the Savior and Lord of the universe. This isn't "true for me" or "true for some" or a "religious preference." It is an unalterable fact. This is the claim of Christian orthodoxy, and it cuts against the grain of the perverse modern understanding of pluralism.

This is the issue. Yet many people fight to avoid the issue entirely. Religious discussions are fine, and dialogue is welcome; but decisions about truth . . . well, that is viewed as going too far. They deem it better to be left in the swamp of current opinions than to reach an island of conviction and certainty. But before the island will look attractive the modern pluralists must see that they are drowning. Everyone may be entitled to his own opinion, but everyone is not entitled to his own truth. Truth is but one.

Modern pluralism presents one prevailing opinion about Jesus Christ. Like all great religious leaders, he is special but not unique; and he is certainly not exclusive. That would be closed- and narrow-minded. He is classed with the multitude of masters, grouped with the gurus, but not exalted as supreme. He is tucked into a comfortable corner of the religious pantheon so as to disturb no one.

The assumption is that Jesus couldn't have claimed to be the only way; that's undemocratic! So instead of facing Christ's challenge as it stands, the whole idea is dismissed as antipluralistic and closed-minded. Pluralism is here used (or abused) to grant a person immunity from investigating the gospel.

But this brand of pluralism is not open-minded. It is closed to the possibility of absolute truth. Professing to consider all options, it will not consider the Christian option: for this "option" claims to tower above all the rest in judgment. This is what G. K. Chesterton called "the illiberality of the liberals."

How, then, can the Christian face the charge of bigotry and closed-mindedness? How can the Christian communicate Christ in a pluralistic age?

First, the open-minded pluralist should be open to investigating the Christian claim of truth. Why should it be necessary to believe that an absolute truth can never be found? That kind of agnosticism takes a hefty dose of (negative) faith—faith in uncertainty itself. Now who is closed-minded?

Second, the idea that all beliefs are relative and that none are absolutely true breaks on the hard rocks of reality. It is blatantly illogical because it is tantamount to saying that there are absolutely no absolutes. It makes an absolute statement in order to assert that there can be no absolute statements. Such "absolute relativism" is self-refuting, a contradiction in terms—and is therefore false.

Third, Christian faith is not a closed-minded faith in the sense of irrationally clinging to ridiculous assumptions, misinterpreting the facts, or engaging in superstition. Rather, it actively applies God's truth to the whole of life. All things are seen in light of God's universal truth. If God is Lord of all, then his truth applies to all of life. As it is often said, "All truth is God's truth." Christians need not cower in a corner of pious unreality. Rather, they can be like Paul who debated the thinkers of his day with confidence and wisdom. As Christ said, the narrow gate leads to life; but from that gate all things are seen in proper perspective. In trying to accept everything in the name of tolerance, the open-minded pluralist precisely loses the power of accepting anything and so becomes intolerant of truth. The modern pluralist is so open-minded his brains fall out.

Fourth, it is not necessarily bigoted or unloving to challenge someone's beliefs. Not to speak the truth is to endorse a lie. The gospel involves radical surgery; it cuts to the heart of the problem, the festering malignancy of sin. Not to wield the scalpel of truth is to condone and support deception. But we must use the scalpel lovingly and not slash away with self-righteous arrogance. While we can know the truth by God's grace, our understanding of it is not infallible. The Bible is inerrant, but we are not.

But we don't need to be infallible to have hope, or to be firm in our conviction of the truth of the uniqueness of Christ and of the gospel. Recognizing the pressures of living in a pluralistic culture can make us more alert yet less defensive to the challenges we face as servants of the truth.

14

The Quest
for Revelation

We all have the will to know, the need for assurance and certainty concerning the crucial issues of life. The question, How should I live my life? goes with the question, Whom should I trust? All our lives are built on one authority or another, depending on which authority wins our trust, answers our questions, and commands our obedience.

In other words, we seek a revelation to lead and guide us. This naturally becomes our standard for judgment, our reference-point and motivation. Inspiration comes from revelation. Christians trust in God and are so motivated and directed by his revelation in Christ and in the Bible. But Christians are not alone in their trust in revelation. Everyone has a "revelation." The question is, Which revelation?

The history of the world could be summarized as "the quest for revelation." Pagan shamans, wizards, and diverse holy men were and are viewed as channels of revelation for the gods and spirits. The oracles of ancient Greece prophesied profundities for the listeners. Mystery religions offered a frenzied ecstasy (induced by drugs, dancing, orgies) to open one to the divine "mysteries" (revelations). Many religious scriptures claim to be the Word of God, the revelation of truth. Politically, in the ancient Near East, a pagan statism declared that king or pharaoh claimed to be God or God's privy spokesman. The king's word was law; from him came revelation.

In the Enlightenment, Jean-Jacques Rousseau (1712–1778) wrote of and popularized a type of "democratic revelation": the voice of the people (majority) is the voice of God (*vox populi, vox dei*). We echo this spirit with our infatuation with opinion polls or what could be called "statistical revelation." The percentages of public opinion become our revelation, our guide and standard. On the totalitarian end, modern authoritarian regimes equate their manmade law with revelation: "The Infallible State has spoken!" The modern pharaohs declare their word.

The modern world of the occult repeats ancient themes for Western consumers, promising direction from astrology, the I Ching, tarot, and the wisdom of "ascended masters" (spirits). Much of "UFO-ology" is fueled by the quest for revelation. But for a word from the star-people, a word of hope for our sick planet from those more highly evolved! We yearn for that "close encounter" of revelation.

Westernized Eastern mysticism tantalizes us with its "God within": Find divinity, goodness, and direction in your deepest Self (God). Much of this is mass marketed as "guru-centered"— for he too is a revelation of the way of inner discovery and bliss.

Even in modern science, despite its studied avoidance of occult credulity, some search for an extraterrestrial disclosure (revelation). The same Carl Sagan who rightly attacked *Chariots of the Gods?* as imbecilic and irrational wrote a popular book called *The Cosmic Connection* (1973) that explored the possibilities of communicating with extraterrestrial intelligences (ETIs). In a later work, Sagan expands on the consequences of such a "cosmic connection": "The practical as well as the philosophical benefits likely to accrue from the receipt of a long message from an advanced civilization are immense." Notice the term *philosophical benefits.* The hope for such a stellar revelation has led Sagan to organize a private group to better the cosmic cause.

At the "frontiers" of science is a popular book, *The Secret Life of Plants* (1973) (later made into a movie), which finds consciousness and potential wisdom in the plant world. . . . Strange tales from the Findhorn community in Scotland report conversations with various nature devas, elves, sprites, elementals and other vegetable verbalizers amidst their New Age agricultural community. *The Oregon Daily Emerald* (12 May 1981) ran a story on Dorothy Maclean, one of the cofounders of Findhorn:

> Dorothy Maclean talks to plants. And they talk back. . . . [She] held her first conversation with the deva [Sanskrit for angel] of the garden pea, the "landscape angel." The deva greeted Maclean and asked what had taken human beings so long to talk to plants.

This pantheistic-animistic world view points to the flora for facts, the hidden facts of revelation. One scene from the movie *The Secret Life of Plants* shows a woman trying to talk to a plant wired for response. One wonders if the reply could have been something as profound as, "Change my fertilizer!"

Much of the current scientific and ecological interest in whales and dolphins is, I think, undertaken because of the quest for revelation. "Interspecies communication" becomes the hope for harmony and peace on the planet. We want to learn from their ways.

The modern psychology of a "culture of narcissism" looks within the self for revelation and wholeness. The appropriate psychoanalytic excavation or psychodynamic technique is able to uncover the revelatory truths locked within. In selfishness we look to the self alone.

All these "revelations" become false gods when viewed as the ultimate authority in life. They cast off restraint by suppressing the true revelation of God. The quest for revelation is futile apart from the perfect revelation of God seen in Christ and the Bible. Yet God redirects the misguided quests of fallen and confused people by his grace and love. He can turn our folly into his glory and work through our errors for his truth. And which of the many contending revelations compares to the incarnation of the God-Man—God made flesh for humanity?

> Who, being in very nature God,
>   did not consider equality with God
>   something to be grasped,
> but made himself nothing,
>   taking the very nature of a servant,
>   being made in human likeness.
> And being found in appearance as a man,
>   he humbled himself
>   and became obedient to death—
>   even death on a cross . . . [Phil. 2:6–8]

And that horrible death on the cross was to set people free from delusion and sin, that they may be forgiven through Christ's atoning sacrifice and that they may be given new life and hope through his resurrection from the dead. Those who respond in repentance and faith are assured of their acceptance before God and are given certain direction revealed through the Spirit and the Word. The quest for revelation has been answered. Let those who know this Revelator bank on his revelation and reveal it to others. Let those with "the will to know" and the need for assurance and certainty turn to the Giver, Sustainer, and Redeemer of life . . . lest they "cast off restraint" forever.

15

Where Do We Go
from Here?
A Pro-Life Call to Arms

Many supporters and activists in the pro-life movement feel dismayed and disheartened by the political stronghold that the pro-abortion forces have established in this country. The question confronts us: Do we give up and retreat from activism into apathy, or do we reconceptualize the restrategize so that the pro-life message can have maximum impact during the Clinton era and beyond? Opting in favor of the latter, I would like first to consider ways in which former pro-life strategies were less than fully effective, and then to explore possible new approaches that will engage and challenge a culture largely desensitized to the tragedy of abortion.

For two decades, a fairly common pro-life view of the abortion debate has been that pro-choice ideology stems from the feminist belief that women ought to be like men and not have to bear children because motherhood is oppressive. This perception—that abortion follows necessarily from feminism because femi-

Rebecca Merrill Groothuis wrote this chapter.

nism is at root opposed to motherhood—has caused many pro-lifers to resist "abortion rights" as part and parcel of feminism. As a result, pro-lifers have been seen as being opposed to women's equality. But this has only added fuel to the modern feminist fire. The cry that opposition to abortion rights constitutes opposition to women's rights has been trumpeted all the more loudly and heard all the more clearly.

To oppose abortion for antifeminist reasons inevitably alienates those in the pro-life camp from all those outside it. If pro-choice people are to relinquish what they perceive to be a right to abortion, they must be persuaded that it need not entail a relinquishment of opportunities for women to participate in the social, cultural, political, and professional arenas. They must be made to see that abortion is wrong—not because it is a means to women's liberation, but because it is a hindrance to women's liberation. They must be made to see that abortion is unjustifiable even as a "woman's right," that fighting for the right to abortion is like fighting for the right to shoot oneself in the foot.

Mainstream feminists perceive the right to abortion as a means to achieving women's equality. So when pro-lifers oppose not only abortion but also the end for which feminists believe abortion is a means, then their persuasive task becomes impossibly large. Pro-lifers are obliged to do more than demonstrate that abortion itself is wrong; they must demonstrate that social equality for women is also wrong. Since such an argument is dismissed by feminists as regressive patriarchalism, pro-choice feminists are left free to continue in an implicit "end justifies the means" ethic: abortion may be undesirable, but it is at times a necessary evil in order that the far greater evil of women's continued oppression be averted. Because the women's-rights-conscious public has been unable to accept the antifeminist pro-life message, pro-lifers have focused more on coercion (through protest and politics) than on persuasion (through education and ministry).

Just as an antifeminist argument for the protection of the unborn falls on deaf ears in a culture that largely supports women's equality, so a pro-life religious argument carries little persuasive power in a pluralistic and secularized society. It too does more to help than to hinder the abortion rights cause, in that it provides opportunity for pro-choicers to dismiss opposition to abortion as a religious issue. They reason that since the state ought not establish religious beliefs but leave such matters to the individual conscience, there are no grounds on which to rule abortion illegal. If a woman's religious beliefs forbid abortion, then it is her choice to continue with an unwanted pregnancy; but if not, then it is her right to choose to abort. It sounds pluralistic, democratic, and individualistic—principles dear to the heart of Americans, to which none dare object.

In habitually preaching to the converted—basing the pro-life argument primarily on antifeminist and religious objections to abortion—pro-lifers not only have missed their audience, but also have provided ample opportunity for pro-choicers to caricature them as narrow-minded religious bigots. But if pro-lifers were to focus on arguments that begin upon the common ground they hold with their opponents—a concern for the legitimate exercise of women's rights, for example—then the pro-choice contingent would be forced to confront their flawed rationale for abortion rights and to engage in productive debate rather than slogan-saturated name-calling. The pro-life movement needs to develop a convincing public voice—a rhetoric appropriate for the marketplace of ideas. It is time to exchange the old, failed tactics for a new, principled pragmatism.

Perhaps God has allowed the advocates of abortion to attain political power in order to impel pro-lifers to do what they ought to have done long ago—to focus on fixing those societal conditions that have made abortion appear to be necessary for the cause of women's equality. First on the agenda of the new pro-life strategy should be establishing an adequate number of crisis pregnancy centers. This step is important not only because it has finally become clear to everyone that the twenty-year pro-life goal of outlawing abortion is not likely to be realized. It is important also because the inadequate number of crisis pregnancy centers—despite the fine efforts of pro-life ministries such as the Christian Action Council—has contributed to the public perception that the abortion option is necessary in order for women to deal with unplanned pregnancies. The lack of social concern for and accommodation to women's needs is part of the problem of which the abortion rights agenda is but a symptom.

With abortion's legality firmly entrenched in the political system, crisis pregnancy centers are certainly needed in order to give women with problem pregnancies the opportunity to make the right choice. Too often women have been given to believe that abortion is their only choice. Pro-life advocates must make the choice for life feasible and available. But because pro-life concern usually has focused more on the life of the fetus than that of the mother, it is likely that if abortion had been made illegal, there would be less pro-life incentive to fund crisis pregnancy centers. What, then, would women do whose pregnancies threatened their livelihood in some way? It is this lopsided emphasis of the mainstream pro-life agenda that has contributed to the movement being pegged as anti-women. The development of many more crisis pregnancy centers must not be viewed as Plan B, to be instituted after having failed at Plan A (outlawing abortion). Even if abortion were illegal, this would not solve the social problems that made legalized abortion appear needful in the first place. It would not make the establishing of crisis pregnancy centers any less crucial.

Conservative pro-lifers, however, have exposed one social problem that fuels the mainstream feminists' insistence on women's right to abortion, namely, the modern ethic of sexual "liberation." It stands to reason that the more frequently sexual relations occur between people who are not permanently committed to one another, the more frequently problem pregnancies are likely to result. And the more such sexual behavior is socially sanctioned, the more frequently it will occur. But even pro-life feminists tend to overlook this illness of society, which also gives rise to the symptom of abortion.

So we need to acknowledge and treat all the societal ills that have created our abortion culture—the sexual permissiveness deplored by the traditional pro-lifers, and the disregard and disrespect for women endemic to social conventions and institutions that are deplored by pro-life feminists.

What, then, are the underlying social problems and inequities that have made abortion appear to be necessary for the cause of women's equality, and how does the practice of abortion actually undercut the feminist concern that women be treated with respect and integrity? First of all, it is clear that the modern ethic of sexual "freedom" places women in a position of greater vulnerability to abuse and oppression by men. The availability of women for casual sex brings out the worst in men and offers the worst for women. Men at their worst view sex as an occasion for an ego-building assertion of male power and dominance, while women tend to view it as an occasion for love and intimacy. It is not difficult to see who is most likely to get hurt by this mismatching of motives.

Feminists who advocate sexual license for women as well as men are simply playing into the hands of the men who seek irresponsible sex with any woman who is momentarily desirable. Women are still sex objects; they are simply more available than they used to be. Women as well as men are routinely denying responsibility for the children they unintentionally conceive—with the help of legalized abortion. Now more than ever, a woman is a pawn in a man's world, a sex object whose use is dictated by the male rules of the sexual game.

Because the "sexually liberated" woman must have recourse to abortion on occasion, she becomes doubly hurt. She is hurt by those men who are more interested in sexual conquest than sexual intimacy and responsibility, and she is hurt when she perceives as necessary the violation of her own body and the killing of her own offspring in abortion—simply to be like men sexually. In sexual liberation, only lust has been liberated; women have remained enslaved.

When feminists declare that women's only hope for freedom and equality is to have the opportunity to abort all unwanted unborn babies, they are giving in to the cultural agenda that accords men the right to impregnate women but absolves them of the responsibility to care for the children they father. The abortion solution agrees that men are not responsible for the children they conceive, and moreover declares that neither are women. Abortion not only kills innocent human life; it keeps the players in the male game playing. It is women's white flag of surrender, saying, we can't beat them so we have joined them.

Abortion does not equalize the unequal; it destroys the unequal. It destroys both women and unborn humans, as well as society's valuation of human life in general and children's lives in particular. Two decades of legalized abortion have not succeeded in according women an equal valuation with men in society. Rather, the devaluation of human life that is basic to the abortion "ethic"—and, indeed, to all forms of bigotry and injustice perpetrated by one group of people against another—has increasingly poisoned every aspect of society. The rate not only of abortion but also of divorce, child abuse, rape, and other forms of violence committed by humans against other humans has been on the rise. This is the abortion culture, in which human life is devalued and therefore deemed disposable—sacrificed on the altar of the needs and desires of the more powerful.

The devaluation of women by a male-oriented society is a part of this picture. The abortion solution plays into the hands of those who maintain that women's work is worth less than the work that men do; that, indeed, a woman's work is valuable only to the extent that it mimics that which traditionally has been deemed men's work. And this, of course, leaves no room for the task of childbearing. Pregnancy is quintessentially women's work and therefore not valued, supported, or rewarded.

A career woman who becomes pregnant must survive simultaneously in two worlds—the "man's world" of work and the woman's world of childbearing. The abortion option stands at the ready, not because she is a liberated career woman, but because, her womanhood being devalued, she is required to be like a man in order to remain in the world of work. Those who determine whether she will be promoted or demoted, retained or let go, reason that because she could choose abortion, her pregnancy is entirely her choice, her problem, for which she and she alone must pay the price. Because the world of work was initially designed to suit the lives of men with "full-time wives," and because such men are concerned with neither pregnancy nor child care, there is no room in the system for women with these concerns. But room needs to be made. Thanks to the abortion mentality, women suffer today, not because they are not allowed into the system, but because they must deny their womanhood in order to be allowed to remain in the system. Women are not given opportunity to do their work as women, but only as surrogate men.

This is not liberation or equality. It is plain, old-fashioned sexism in a new guise, and the implementation of abortion rights is its primary proponent and perpetrator. Although this new sexism allows women to be the same as men where they are the same (in their ability to make valuable contributions to society in various arenas), it does not allow women to be—or value them for being—different where they are different. The male is still the norm, and woman is still less than man. Her difference is her deviance—a "problem" that abortion "solves." In the old sexism, women were encouraged to marry and bear children, but they were allowed only to bear children; their other abilities were denied and they were barred from significant contribution to society in other respects. Their womanhood denied them equality. Now, "equality" has denied them their womanhood. Womanhood is still deemed less valuable than manhood, in that whenever its functions are operative a woman loses her "equality." She can be treated equally (like a man) as long as she doesn't act like a woman and have a baby. The prospect of dealing with pregnancy in a workplace designed for men can be so daunting that a woman may feel a need to resort to abortion, the final solution in a society that devalues both women and the human life they bear. But women's choices, opportunities, and responsibilities ought to reflect the reality of where women and men are alike, as well as where they are unlike.

The modern feminist advocacy of abortion rights is self-defeating and logically inconsistent in many other ways. It constitutes a significant deviation from the nineteenth-century feminists' opposition to abortion. These women believed that abortion serves as a means of male oppression against women and their children. Yet modern feminists bill themselves as the faithful followers of those early feminists. Moreover, abortion is undeniably an act of violence; and feminists deplore the "male" means of problem-solving whereby the powerful exact violence against the powerless. Yet mainstream feminists unhesitatingly advocate the violent destruction of the powerless unborn as a solution to the problem of an unwanted pregnancy.

Advocates of abortion rationalize that the unborn baby is not an individual with rights, but is merely part of the mother's body, over which she has absolute right of ownership. Such an argument slides glibly over the distinction of being *part* of the mother's body and being *in* the mother's body; the latter does not necessarily entail the former. But even according to the (false) definition of the fetus as merely part of the mother's body, abortion must be seen as an act of violence a woman perpetrates against her own body, bringing a brutal end to a natural bodily process that would otherwise bring new life to birth.

Making the child entirely the property of its mother not only gives her the right to destroy her child, but also relieves the child's father of all parental obligation. If the father has no claim on or rights to his child before it is born, he can easily and logically abdicate responsibility for his child after it is born. Insisting that every woman has a choice whether to continue or to terminate a pregnancy has the same effect. On this basis, the father of an unplanned-for, unborn child can disavow all responsibility to both woman and child other than to offer to pay for an abortion. If the woman refuses to abort her baby, then it is deemed entirely her choice to have the child and consequently entirely her responsibility to care for the child. The pro-choice argument subverts the feminist ideal of co-parenting, which is based upon the conviction that the father's duty to care and provide for his children is no less than the mother's. Women will never enjoy equal vocational opportunity unless men are willing to assume equal parental responsibility. Again it is apparent that the abortion rights agenda ultimately undermines the cause for women's equality.

Nonetheless, mainstream feminists doggedly insist that women have no hope of equality or justice unless they have the right to destroy their unborn offspring at will. Such thinking capitulates to the assumption that only those who conform to the traditional male lifestyle are free to pursue their own desires and vocational goals. But to the extent that women measure their liberty according to how closely they are able to approximate this lifestyle, they seek a false equality. They seek to be equal where they are not nor can be equal, and such an endeavor can only injure women because it denies part of their essential identity.

Feminists ought instead to be trying to create a society that not only respects women as persons who, like men, have a variety of vocational abilities to offer the world, but also respects women's unique gift of bearing new life. Such a society would accommodate women in this process instead of punishing them vocationally, economically, and socially when pregnancy occurs. It is to the advantage of both pro-lifers and feminists to initiate the sort of social reforms that will encourage and enable women to choose life for their unborn children. Abortion is not a solution to women's social inequality; rather, the fact that it is perceived as a solution is itself an indication or a symptom of women's inequality, the perpetuation of which abortion encourages rather than eliminates.

The objective of any legitimate movement for equality is to equalize an unjust (undeserved and unjustifiable) relationship of inequality between two classes of people by endowing the underprivileged class with the basic human and civil rights enjoyed by the privileged class. This action inevitably results in the loss of many of the privileged class's privileges, because those privileges were maintained by the denial of equal rights to the underprivileged class. White people, for example, no longer have easy recourse to underpaid domestic help. This is because black people have been accorded some of the basic human and civil rights enjoyed by white people. The subjugation of the entire class of black people was too high a price to pay for the privileges it offered the class of white people.

Feminists employ the same logic with regard to male privilege and female subordination. For example, a man who has a wife suited for activities other than childcare and household service ought to contribute to these tasks so that she can devote some of her time to other concerns. This is considered a trade-off that helps equalize that which would otherwise be inequitable.

But mainstream feminists today have established, for the sake of their own privilege, a state of inequity between women and the unborn. The class of unborn humans has been stripped of all inherent rights, beginning with the most basic—the right to life.

This class of humans is entirely at the mercy of the privileged class, in whose bodies they reside. If the privileged class wants them to live, they are cared for with the same respect and concern for their health and well-being that anyone on the other side of the womb receives. But if the privileged class does not desire them to live, they are poisoned and/or torn asunder. This is the worst sort of oppression any class of humans could possibly inflict on another class of humans. The idea of abortion rights is premised on the same principles of prejudice and oppression that "justify" the actions of any privileged class that devalues for its own purposes the powerless members of society. Yet it is done in the name of women's equality. The cause purportedly is justice and liberty for the oppressed.

Feminists object to a valuation of woman according to the desirability of her body or the usefulness of her services to some man; rather, feminists insist, a woman has intrinsic value that exists independently of male approval. Yet this is the same standard of bigotry by which mainstream feminists judge the unborn. Apart from its desirability or usefulness to its mother, the unborn baby is granted no value, no rights, no life of its own. The rationale behind a woman's right to abortion bears an ominous resemblance to the rationale for male supremacy and female subjugation.

The abortion rights agenda fights inequality of one form with inequality of another. In shooting at one double standard it uses another double standard as a weapon. It fights for rights for one class by denying rights to another. It is founded upon that which it seeks to destroy, and thereby preserves social injustice rather than destroys it.

When women advocate abortion as the answer to unplanned pregnancy, they are succumbing to the ever-present danger of the oppressed: as they become liberated from their oppressors, they become like their oppressors and thereby abdicate their hard-won liberty from systems of injustice and oppression. When the oppressed appropriate the ways of thinking by which their oppressors justified *their* actions, surely the effect will boomerang: those who seek liberation will reinstitute their own enslavement.

If we in the pro-life movement can persuade those concerned for the rights and needs of women that we share their concern, that we are opposed to oppression in any form, and that it will not harm but rather help the cause for women's rights to seek pro-life solutions to unplanned pregnancies, then our message will stand a better chance of being heard and heeded.

16

Religion, the State, and Endowing the Arts

A lecture I attended in the summer of 1992 ingeniously encapsulated almost all the errors in current thinking about the precarious and recently contentious relationship between religion, the arts, and civil government. The offending orator was John Frohnmayer, who, before his well-publicized exorcism, was chairman of the National Endowment for the Arts (NEA) when it came under heavy fire for funding works that many people considered offensive if not blasphemous. A consideration of Frohnmayer's apologetic for state funding of the arts serves as a foil for further reflections on the matter, a matter not likely to fade away as long as the NEA is itself endowed with fiduciary functions.

Frohnmayer's explanation of the relationship of religion and politics, which sadly typifies much political thinking, set the tone for his later argument for federal support of the arts. He first decried the 1992 Republican platform for mentioning God, then cited the First Amendment as prohibiting such zealotry. The kingdom of God, said Frohnmayer, is "an intellectual and not a political kingdom." But the final blow against religious meddling in public policy was delivered by none other than Reinhold Niebuhr, whom Frohnmayer quoted as saying that the danger of mixing politics with religion is that it introduces the absolute into the world of relative values.

Frohnmayer, like so many other strict separationists, seeks to separate religious beliefs and principles from public life instead of separating ecclesiastical institutions from public establishment. The latter is the intention and plain meaning of the First Amendment; the former is an eisegetical aberration that restricts freedom of religion to merely private forms of expression. Christianity certainly is, as Frohnmayer says, "an intellectual kingdom." But this fact does not restrict its relevance to the personal and subjective realm; rather it extends its relevance, because Christianity is a world view that speaks to every area of life, private and public. One wonders if Frohnmayer would censure Thomas Jefferson's prologue to the Declaration of Independence for mixing religion and politics by affirming that humans are endowed by the Creator with certain inalienable rights. That theological endowment has both religious and political applications.

As for Frohnmayer's reference to Niebuhr, we have to wonder if he didn't speak ill of the dead. Niebuhr did warn against the utopianism project of absolutizing any political ideology (religious or secular), yet he was far from being the rank relativist Frohnmayer's selective quotation intimated; neither did he desire to limit religious expression to an intellectual ghetto. Had he so wished, he would have had to muzzle himself as a religious thinker tempted to make political judgments. He did not do so, and those who either feast or glean from his political observations are in his debt—incautious invocations notwithstanding.

If this critique is familiar territory to my readers, I might be excused by quoting George Orwell: "We have now sunk to a depth at which the restatement of the obvious is the first duty of the intelligent man." But beyond this dutiful restatement of the obvious, I want to explore how Frohnmayer's all-too-common misunderstanding of fundamental issues affects the matter of public funding of the arts.

The bulk of Frohnmayer's apologetic focused on why the state should support the arts. He reasoned that worthwhile art may not be self-supporting, at least in it nascent stages. And if not for federal support, the likes of Garrison Keillor, Spike Lee, and Geena Davis may have never graced the artistic scene. This, of course, is a counterfactual statement that must remain forever unprovable. It seems more likely that such talent would rise to the top even without federal support. Such would not be without precedent, given the fact that the arts have long thrived before national endowments.

Moreover, Frohnmayer stated that federal funding of the arts can encourage economic development when unknowns become well known through public support and then are successful enough to generate industry in their wake. This economic boon may occur in a small number of cases, but much of what the NEA supports is too avant-garde and experimental to be translated into any economic cornucopia. The ethos of much of the art funded by the NEA militates against commercial success. Consider, for example, the commercial potential of the depiction of a crucifix submerged in urine.

One of Frohnmayer's examples of beneficial state funding of the arts was particularly ironic. He observed that neither the pyramids of Egypt nor the Great Wall of China (great works of art worthy of existence) were constructed through private enterprise; rather, these endeavors required state support. Although I can't speak about the Great Wall of China, the Egyptian pyramids were not state-funded in the modern, bureaucratic sense. They were state-mandated by a despot through the conscription of tens of thousands of state workers (better known in our day as slaves). The Egyptians were notoriously inept at separating church and state. The pyramids were religious monuments from base to peak, and built through taxpayer expense and state labor!

The kind of religious folk that Frohnmayer and his cohorts would summarily relegate to political muteness are concerned that state support of the arts could result in a similar situation on a smaller scale—call it statism—where the funds of religious citizens are used for purposes violently at odds with their fundamental beliefs. Pyramids or no, the state qua state wields the military and financial sword: it alone can legally extract funds upon threat of violence and incarceration; it alone can governmentally allocate those extracted funds according to legal policy. Wielding the sword is not illegitimate (if the apostle Paul is to be trusted), so long as it cuts where and when it ought and remains safely in the scabbard the rest of the time.

I raised the matter of funding objectionable artistic material to Frohnmayer in a written question: "According to what legal and moral principle did you justify the use of public funds to finance work that depicts Christ as a drug addict when this deeply offends the sensibilities and beliefs of millions of taxpaying Americans?" The work to which I referred shows an agonized Christ with a hypodermic needle in his vein.

Frohnmayer's response was telling, and representative of much of present political thinking. The work I mentioned, he said, was only a small part of a larger collage. This, I suppose, means that because of its diminutive dimension it ought not offend. But if a piece of art that depicted Martin Luther King as a drug addict happened to be part of a larger collage, would this make it any less offensive to the modern sensibility? Frohnmayer noted that the religious zealots who objected to depicting Christ as a drug addict did not see it in its proper setting and so had not "encountered the art work." This rendered their (philistinian) judgment unworthy of consideration.

Frohnmayer's final move was to castigate the religious objectors as poor theologians. He informed the audience of two theological propositions that exonerated the piece from committing blasphemy. First, according to orthodox theology, Christ died for our sin. Second, drug addiction is a sin. Therefore, the depiction represents Christ dying for the sins of drug addicts. This is a classic non sequitur. Orthodox theology indeed confesses that Jesus paid the penalty for human sin on the cross. But it emphatically denies that Christ committed any sin, drug-related or otherwise. To picture Christ as a drug addict is to involve him in committing sin. This rudimentary consideration explodes the supposed orthodoxy of the depiction or, at best, makes any traditional religious meaning it might convey so esoteric as to be undetectable.

Another irony in Frohnmayer's rationale for the work is that if the artistic depiction served Christian orthodoxy, it should have never received federal funds, given Frohnmayer's view of the strict separation between church and state.

But deeper concerns emerge upon reflecting on Frohnmayer's response. He assumes, as do many unelected officials with substantial endowing powers, that the tastes and sensibilities of the common person, especially the common religious person, are irrelevant to the dispensations of the federal government. This was highlighted by Frohnmayer's comments that the NEA should not be accountable to Congress for how it allocates its funds because we must "let art be art" without political tinkering. This comment seems strange in light of an earlier complaint by Frohnmayer about Dan Quayle's condemnation of the cultural elite in America. Frohnmayer maintained that there are no cultural elites in a democracy (a statement that would scandalize not a few sociologists). But isn't it an elitism of the worst kind for an unaccountable, unelected commission of federal appointees to determine the distribution of millions of dollars to artists who lack sustenance apart from the largesse of the state?

Frohnmayer and his followers here generate another irony. On the one hand, they declare their desire that art be free from the censorious scrutiny of the Jesse Helmses and the Donald Wildmons of the world because we must "let art be art." On the other hand, they insist that art need be federally funded. This in one stroke simultaneously politicizes art to the maximum and removes it from any public accountability. Risking an anachronism, we might call that "taxation without representation" (at least for the nonsubsidized, taxpaying majority).

If we rejected Frohnmayer's apology for state funding of the arts as contradictory, ironic, and elitist, what guidelines should govern public policy in this controversy? I suggest three principles.

First, government funds, whether federal, state, or local, should not support art works that offend the religious sensibilities and beliefs of any established religious community or tradition. This principle may be difficult to implement in a pluralistic setting, but it is an ideal worth pursuing because it is grounded ethically in a basic civility, and legally in the First Amendment: to support offensive material is to restrict the free exercise of religion by requiring religious citizens to subsidize that which they believe to undermine their religious beliefs. Not surprisingly, the best and simplest way to implement this principle is to abolish the NEA entirely, but before that glad day an application of this principle could serve to curb some of the indiscretions of the endowers.

Second, art can and should flourish when left to its own ingenuity and resourcefulness. Artists throughout history have sought and found the favor of private patrons or have produced art while earning a living through other means. The modern image of the artist as the alienated critic of all established order who must not be condemned to a sentence of gainful employment is less than morally axiomatic. The historic American work ethic need not be suspended for the artistically gifted. The tradition of the artisan as an employed laborer in artistic endeavor who provides useful services needs to be revived and cultivated.

Third, if people of faith chafe at the indiscretions of the NEA, let them reinvigorate the arts within and through their own religious institutions so as to offset alien usurpers. The intrusion of the state into the realm of art is partially due to an aesthetic lacuna left by the church. From Michelangelo to Bach, the Western heritage displays a great wealth of art inspired by religious ideals and supported by the church. As the church and other religious institutions have tended to recede into the cultural background, the foreground has been claimed by secular and secularizing forces, not excluding the state itself. This artistic imbalance should be rectified.

John Frohnmayer is no longer chairman of the NEA, although he has, to no one's surprise, written a book about his eminent ouster and the egregious errors of his accusers. Yet the NEA continues to receive and allocate federal funds, and its coffers are likely to swell under the Clinton administration. As long as it endures, it will or at least should stir controversy. We can hope that as long as it exists it will soundly reject the arrogance and illogic of those who seek to marginalize the concerns of religious citizens by exempting publicly funded art from public scrutiny.

17

Sports and American Character

The apostle Peter warns us that "a man is a slave to whatever has mastered him" (2 Pet. 2:19). But the things that overcome us may be so subtle that we barely detect them, much less disarm them. We can be overcome almost unaware, and enslaved implicitly—as perhaps we have been by one of our most acceptable American pastimes.

Our response to sports reveals our cultural character. Our attitude toward recreation shows our values, what we prize and esteem—as did the Romans' worship of games two millennia past. Although we've yet to make sport of literally throwing Christians to lions, our fanatical myopia about sports bespeaks something seriously wrong.

The general character of professional athletes has radically changed, but their status as role models for youth has not. A few years ago the idea of spiking a football, giving a "high five," or taking bows after home runs would have been greeted with jeers, not cheers. Self-congratulation was judged egotistical and unbecoming of athletes. Good sportsmanship—involving humility, team spirit, and self-discipline—was the thing honored. Can you imagine Joe DiMaggio giving a high five after another splendid performance? But today, the aura of honor is replaced by the badge of pride.

Worse yet, temper tantrums, fighting, and out-and-out riots seem to be almost encouraged. Team brawls—whether in baseball, football, or hockey—excite fans more than team victories. Hockey sticks slap bodies as often as pucks. Thus the dark joke, "I saw a fight the other day, and a hockey game broke out." Baseball managers boast of their ejections from games. Vainglory replaces shame. Competition becomes combat. And many of us sit enthralled.

Today's sports uniforms are also revealing (a double meaning *is* intended). Compare the old, baggy baseball uniforms with the new, skin-tight styles. Clearly more than comfort is the issue. The athlete often poses as an exhibitionistic icon, the personification of physical perfection. What could be called "the religion of the healthy body" pays homage at the athlete's feet. Bodily excellence replaces moral excellence, and a good body coupled with a good season more than makes up for a suspension because of a drug bust.

Fans have also changed. We are often no longer content to shut up during our national anthem and wait before cheering our team. We crave immediate gratification, not bothering to show even a minimal amount of respect for our country. Neither do we respect the players. We may adore their successes (statistics being the ultimate standard), but cheers turn quickly and viciously to boos after a poor performance, and team brawls often involve fans as well. We are fairweather fans. Immediate gratification replaces loyalty as the highest value.

Sports is one of the most central and visible elements in American life. In a 1984 issue of *Quill*, a magazine for journalists, Terry Mattingly commented that while Americans spend more time and money on religious pursuits than on sports, the media dedicate the majority of their space to sports. In any newspaper, compare the size of the sports section with the religion page.

Mattingly notes that the Associated Press (AP) and United Press International (UPI) assign one reporter each to religion news for the whole country. He says: "When thousands of sports fans— spending millions of dollars—flock to the nation's stadiums or sit in front of their television sets, hundreds of writers and photographers go with them. When millions of Americans—spending billions of dollars—go to places of worship or sit in front of their television sets, AP's George Cornell and UPI's David Anderson go it alone."

Sports wins the spotlight; and the spotlight often reveals less than Christian character. But these pastimes can so easily become our passions—our obsessions—and our recreations become counterfeit religions. Mantra-like cheers are mystically intoned to aid our side. Blessings and cursings fill the stadiums, arenas, fields, and living rooms. Sporting events are attended with sacramental regularity and devotion. Amusement can turn to addiction, with the trusty cable hook-up tantalizing us with a smorgasbord of every sport under the sun, from karate to canoeing, from bowling to curling, from the Olympics to mud wrestling.

Through such religious devotion, we can be overcome by the vainglory, egotism, and idolatry that poison much of modern sports. (There are, we must inject, blessed exceptions.) Our diversions command our dedication and so divert us from deeper concerns. Our inner life can be strangled by an addiction to the vicarious. We become psychological spectators, alienated from our own being. Sports is an escape. As Blaise Pascal pointed out in *Pensées,* diversions console our miseries, but can distract us from preparing to avoid the greatest misery. Because diversion is that which "prevents us thinking about ourselves and leads us imperceptibly to destruction. But for that we should be bored, and boredom would drive us to seek some more solid means of escape, but diversion passes our time and brings us imperceptibly to our death."[1]

As the barbarians began sacking Rome, the games went on. The fans cheered and jeered, oblivious to reality. Titillation dulled their senses to the sounds of death hammering at the gates. We must discern: Is it doing the same to us?

18

The War after the War
Reflections on the Gulf War

America had gone to war and won. The United States had handily defeated an infamous enemy with firm resolve, military genius, and relatively light casualties. The nation was united in the cause and our president was at the apex of his popularity. Patriotism ran high, flags waved, and the returning troops were welcomed as heroes. America was proud again—at last.

For weeks we saw Baghdad's night sky aglow with streaking missiles and smart bombs; Iraqi SCUD missiles intercepted in a blaze of pyrotechnical precision; oil-drenched birds in Saudi Arabia; instant military celebrities such as Norman Schwarzkopf; tens of thousands of Iraqis surrendering to the nearest allied personnel available (and even to some reporters); and elated Kuwaitis embracing the nearest American available.

In the wake of this fast-moving, highly televised six-week war, we should stop and reflect on the welter of images with which we were bombarded. What exactly happened and how can we respond to it?

126

A Just War or Just a War?

President George Bush argued that the war with Iraq met the classical criteria of the just-war doctrine. I found this impressive. Bush drew on a developed ethical tradition substantially shaped by Christian thinkers through the ages, beginning with Augustine. Briefly, the criteria for launching a just war are

Just cause: The war must have noble motives such as the protection or defense of human life and liberty. Wars of territorial aggression, reprisal, or economic profit are ruled out. If the United States had gone to war primarily because of its thirst for oil, the cause would not be just.

Competent authority: War must be instigated and implemented by legitimate governmental leaders and under the proper legal structure. Paul teaches in Romans 13:1–7 that governing authorities are established by God and have recourse to force.

Comparative justice: If one side's cause is more just than that of its enemies, war is permissible for that side.

Right intention: A war should aim at justice and peace, not vengeance or punishment. Blaise Pascal noted that "might without right is tyrannical."[1]

Last resort: All peaceful means of resolving the conflict must be exhausted. Diplomacy, sanctions, and threats must utterly fail before war is waged.

Probability of success: A just war must be viewed as plausibly winnable. Otherwise, the effort would be futile and the destruction unjustifiable. As Pascal said, "right without might is helpless."[2]

Proportionality of projected results: The projected good effects of the war must exceed its likely ill effects. No one should destroy a country in order to save it.

Right spirit: War should be engaged with an attitude of regret. In other words, a nation should not glory in the war but view it as a necessary evil.

The criteria for waging a just war involve

Proportionality in the use of force: Overkill must be avoided and harm balanced with the good likely to be achieved. Saddam

Hussein's torching of Kuwaiti oil fields, to give just one example, flagrantly violated this principle.

Discrimination: Noncombatants must not be deliberately targeted for military purposes. Noncombatant deaths are probably unavoidable in war, but they should be kept to an absolute minimum. Consider Saddam's indiscriminate targeting by SCUD missiles of civilians in Israel and elsewhere.

Avoidance of evil means: No war justifies torturing or killing prisoners, taking hostages, tormenting civilians, or desecrating holy places. Need I mention Iraq's blatant violation of this principle?

Good faith: Enemies should be treated as human beings and with as much dignity as possible in wartime conditions with the hope of eventual reconciliation in a postwar environment.[3]

It does seem, given the above principles, that our cause and conduct was relatively just. In a fallen world, no war can be without injustice on both sides; yet the magnitude of the evils involved surely shows the allied forces have been in the right, both in launching and in waging the war. (Of course in a real sense, the war was started by Iraq when it invaded Kuwait in August 1990, and when it refused to leave by the 15 January 1991 deadline.)

The fact that Bush invoked the just-war tradition speaks well of his ethical orientation. It also highlights the decisive role that Christian thinkers have played in international ethics over the centuries.

If our cause and conduct was relatively just, how should we feel about America in 1991?

Beyond the War

We should rejoice over the expulsion of Iraq from Kuwait, our comparatively light losses, and the unity of Americans in the cause. We should, in fact, thank God for it. Bush implored us to pray throughout the war but thanked everyone but God in his postwar address before Congress. He did, as a patriotic exclamation point, say "God bless America" in concluding the speech. God's blessing ought not be divorced from our thanksgiving.

Whatever our military success might mean in a highly unstable region of the world, the primacy of evangelism should be kept in view. The spiritual battle for the souls of men and women should not be eclipsed by the physical battles for land and political liberty. The anguish of the Arab soul must be spiritually treated. Although the Arab world has resisted the gospel for centuries, lives can still be changed by the touch of grace—but not without messengers. Let us, then, redouble our efforts to bring Christ to those under the Islamic crescent. The Gulf War has moved me to begin to pray for a brave friend who is risking much to penetrate the Arab world with the light of the gospel.

Mourning is in order for the tragedy that every war inevitably is. We'll never know how many tens of thousands of Iraqis were killed and wounded, nor the suffering of their bereaved loved ones. The American casualties weren't light for the families of those who came home wrapped in the flag rather than waving it. We were largely spared the images of battered corpses and brutalized survivors. Those on the scene were not. As James said, war is ugly because it is born out of sin. "What causes wars, and what causes fightings among you? Is it not your passions that are at war in your members? You desire and do not have; so you kill. And you covet and cannot obtain; so you fight and wage war. You do not have because you do not ask" (James 4:1–2 RSV).

A reasoned patriotism is healthy for national life, and patriotism courses through a celebrating citizenry. But an uncritical nationalism defies the fact that God alone is the moral Lawgiver and Judge of every nation, bar none. He alone is the source, standard, and stipulator of what is good, right, just, and virtuous—not the nation, not the ruler. As Isaiah said: "Surely the nations are like a drop in the bucket; they are regarded as dust on the scales; he weighs the islands as though they were fine dust" (Isa. 40:15).

America, by God's grace, may approximate goodness and justice but it will never define these qualities. It may wage a just war, yet fail to be justified as blameless before the holy audience of God. As G. K. Chesterton noted, "if we boast of our best, we must repent of our worst. Otherwise patriotism will be a very poor thing indeed."[4]

The war also rattled our relativism. In a pluralistic society that often excuses moral aberration as mere personal preference, Saddam Hussein was rightly regarded as evil. There is no excusing his behavior, and that is not just a matter of opinion. There is but one correct opinion: Those who routinely torture and murder the innocent and invade peaceful neighbors are morally malignant. They must be held accountable.

But a stunning military victory over an evil dictator does not a virtuous nation make. We may feel much better about ourselves than we have in decades, but so may a man about to drop from a massive coronary. Despite its historic greatness, America is morally sick and in need of the cure that only revival and reformation can provide. Consider our ills.

Our military used supersophisticated technology to zero in on military targets and avoid civilian casualties. But medical technology claims the lives of more than a million civilians each year through abortion. Fetuses are targeted and destroyed by the "high-tech" weapons of the abortionist. We save lives abroad. We take them at home. Iraqi prisoners of war are treated more humanely than over a million developing human beings have been each year since 1973. If we prayed daily for the war, are we praying for justice for the unborn? The war against Iraq is over; but are we doing anything to stop this unjust war against the weak? We must not forget that "the LORD hates . . . hands that shed innocent blood" (Prov. 6:16–17).

While we feel morally elevated after our victory in a just war with Iraq, America is morally debased in its war with the fallen flesh. American standards of decency are at an all-time low. The rap group 2 Live Crew obscenely glories in all manner of debauchery and escapes criminal charges. Their recordings also go platinum. Pornography receives federal funding from the National Endowment for the Arts. "Artists" routinely desecrate holy objects through their perverse depictions and thereby wage an unjust war against Christian sensibilities. A spineless Congress then cosmetically addresses the public outcry but refuses to disband or discipline the NEA for its promiscuous funding. The vulgarians remain endowed—by our tax dollars.

In our churches, doctrinal discernment ranges from minimal to nonexistent. The flock often falls prey to secular trends because it is neither well-grounded in biblical theology nor are aware of the dynamic of spiritual combat with fallen forces. As theologian and apologist R. C. Sproul has observed, we live in the most anti-intellectual era of church history. We have little to say to a decaying culture because our minds are not engaged by the Mind of minds, the Lord God all-knowing and all mighty. We are largely content with a trivial and shallow religion that lacks the intellectual and moral nerve required to voice truth and stand tall against error both within and without the church. Why doesn't the world listen to us? Because we say little worth hearing.

I could go on. So could you. I've diagnosed only a few of our many maladies. But there are also pockets of hope and life. God is not without his soldiers, and he reigns despite our national nightmares. His throne is not shaken by our inequities, though we may be shaken to the foundations. We have seen the speck in Iraq's eye, and we have rightly deemed war against it to be just. Will we now have the discernment and the courage to see—and remove—the log in our own eye? Our victory abroad may little console us if we are defeated at home—by ourselves.

19

Ancient Assistance
Against the New Age

An insightful poster reads: "There are two important facts about the universe: (1) There is a God; (2) You are not he." This is Christianity in a nutshell. The Creator God is not confused with creation. Humans are not now, nor will they ever be, divine. God is a personal being, not an impersonal principle, force, or essence.

A New Age version of this poster would read: "There are two important facts about the universe: (1) There is a God; (2) You are it." Or, in the words of Joseph Campbell (from the television series and book *The Power of Myth*): "You are God, not in your ego, but in your deepest being, where you are at one with the nondual transcendent." This is the heart of New Age spirituality: people are divine and must rediscover this potential in order to better the world.

Old Roots of the New Age

G. K. Chesterton, Christian apologist par excellence, observed in 1930 that "we hear much about new religions; many

132

of them based on the very latest novelties of Buddha and Pythagoras."[1] The perennial war of ideas develops few new weapons systems. In the intellectual combat between the New Age movement and orthodox Christianity, the points of conflict were recognized by the early church eighteen hundred years before New Age celebrity evangelist Shirley MacLaine spoke to her first disembodied spirit.

Prophets of the New Age such as Campbell frequently hark back to Gnosticism for spiritual inspiration, saying that people can live out of the sense of Christ in them, as Jesus lived out of the Christhood of his nature. Campbell quotes from the Gnostic text The Gospel of Thomas to the effect that Jesus' mission was to reveal the deity of all people.

Of course, as New Age leaders imbibe at the well of gnosis, they strain out what offends modernity's tastes. The harsh Gnostic dualism of dark matter versus pure Spirit is ignored or redefined in psychological terms. The fantastic hierarchic cosmologies of innumerable spiritual beings are likewise winked at or interpreted, in good Jungian form, as manifestations of psychological processes.

Yet the ancient appeal of Gnosticism remains: There is a hidden and secret wisdom (*gnosis*) that can be directly experienced by turning within. This gnosis is not found in traditional orthodoxy, which is merely esoteric or external, but in the deeper or esoteric meaning. The supreme realization of gnosis is the spark of divinity within. Underneath the illusions of ignorance burns the fire of the unlimited.

Irenaeus, Heresy Fighter

The exact origins of Gnosticism are a matter of scholarly debate, but we find it thriving as an alternative to orthodox Christianity in the second century, and several New Testament writers such as John and Paul may have been responding to Gnostic or proto-Gnostic elements in their letters.

The greatest apologist against the Gnostics was the early church theologian Irenaeus, who wrote *Against Heresies* in approximately A.D. 180. This work illustrates several principles for dealing with the neo-Gnostic or New Age teachings so widespread today.

Irenaeus went to great lengths properly to identify and explain the beliefs of the "Gnostics so-called." Against Heresies presents a careful analysis of the Gnostic system in its different forms. Until the discovery of many primary Gnostic texts near Nag Hammadi, Egypt, in the 1940s, Irenaeus and other apologists provided nearly all of scholars' knowledge of the Gnostics. (Although some have disparaged the church fathers' treatments, historian Patrick Henry observes that they have integrity and "it is still legitimate to use [their] materials to characterize Gnosticism."[2]) Irenaeus, while opposing Gnosticism as a world view antithetical to Christianity, labored to fairly present its views. No matter how ridiculous or blasphemous Christians find various New Age teachings, caricature is never an appropriate apologetic.

Irenaeus recognized and countered the Gnostics' biblical misinterpretation. Gnostics defended any number of unbiblical doctrines by appealing to scriptural texts out of context and with no respect for the authors' intent. Irenaeus realized the Gnostic teachers "gather their views from other sources than the Scriptures" while "they endeavor to adapt with an air of probability to their own peculiar assertions the parables of the Lord, the sayings of the prophets, and the words of the apostles." Irenaeus says this eisegesis "disregards the order and connection of the Scriptures." He likens this to taking apart the individual jewels that make up a skilled artist's beautiful image of a king and rearranging them so as to make them into a dog or a fox.

When cults twist biblical texts in service of their message, their literary license needs to be unmasked.

Irenaeus attacked the irrationality of Gnostic theology. In one memorable passage, he lampoons the common Gnostic claim that the ultimate godhead is absolutely unknowable and unnameable. The apologist finds it odd that the Gnostics speak so much and with such metaphysical gusto about that which, on their own terms, they can neither know anything nor say anything about! Since the Gnostics assign a wide variety of names to spiritual principles that they take to be unnameable, Irenaeus proposes his own cluster of ultimate spiritual entities: Gourd, Utter-Emptiness, Cucumber, and Melon! Irenaeus's satire spotlights the stupidity of making the absolute reality beyond all words or thoughts.

When, for example, Campbell asserts in *The Power of Myth* that "God is beyond names and forms" and even "transcends thingness" (and later goes on to say all sorts of things about the God who cannot be known!),[3] it is wise to remember and demonstrate the rank illogic of such remarks.

Irenaeus kept Christology at the center of his work. Irenaeus knew that the Gnostic distortion of the meaning and work of Jesus Christ was its most dangerous aspect. Gnostics, then as now, divide the man Jesus from "the Christ" in various ways.

In one approach, the Christ was viewed as a spirit that temporarily visited Jesus and left him at the cross. Irenaeus realized that this perversion of Jesus leaves people fast in their fallen state because it denies that Christ died for sins.

Another Gnostic view held that Jesus as an enlightened man was visited by the same Christ that elicits the Christhood in each person. To this Irenaeus responded, "The Gospel . . . knew of no other man but him who was of Mary, who also suffered; and no Christ who flew away from Jesus before the passion; but him who was born it knows as Jesus Christ the Son of God, and that this same suffered and rose again."

New Age teachings offer variations of these ancient errors: Jesus is a man who tapped into a universal Christ consciousness; or he is an example of what a self-realized master can do. Modern-day apologists must imitate Irenaeus, who lifted up the Jesus of biblical revelation in the face of these confusions.

Heresies will remain until the end, but new heresies are hard to find indeed. The Gnostic planks of self-deification, biblical distortion, irrationality, and christological confusion are mirrored in the neo-Gnostic elements of the New Age movement. With an eye toward Irenaeus, contemporary Christians can discover principles of confrontation just as applicable today as they were eighteen hundred years ago.

20

Beyond the Perfect Compost Pile

One rather maddening feature of modernity is its frenetically protean propensities. Cultural and religious movements are often in a condition of almost constant flux. To steal from Heraclitus, it often seems that you can't step into the same movement twice. Although there is permanence in the basic philosophical fundaments of world view—metaphysical perspectives are not unlimited—social movements adapt, revise, and renew themselves in a dizzying assortment of ways. "New and improved" models greet us almost daily. Images change and face-lifts abound.

Partially because of its adaptability, the much discussed, much underestimated, and much overestimated New Age movement has been difficult to get a fix on sociologically. But one key to its interpretation is found in a magazine started in 1975 called, appropriately enough, *New Age Journal*. The messianic and millennial force of the name was indicative of a post-countercultural remnant vying for social survival in the hope for eventual spiritual and social transformation. It was the "Aquarian Age" on hold.

Most of the journal's articles from 1975 to the early eighties were aimed at an enlightened few who, while no longer incorporated into a visible counterculture, retained New Age sensibilities (if not credal confessions): the sentiments of the New Left; post-Christian, pantheistic predilections; and a lingering utopianism waiting its turn.

Thus, *New Age Journal* was a forum for transplanted gurus (like Rajneesh and Muktananda), scientists-cum-mystics (like physicist Fritjof Capra), spiritual ecologists (like Gregory Bateson), leftist politicos gone spiritual (like Mark Satin and Jerry Rubin), endless avant-garde therapies (all traveling through the Esalen Institute at one time or another), neopagan feminists (like Starhawk), New Age social critics (like William Irwin Thompson and Theodore Roszak), and not a few organic gardeners who equated nirvana (roughly) with the perfect compost pile.

By the mid-eighties *New Age Journal* began to take on a new look, both in content and style. It became slick. The pages were brighter, smoother, and more colorful; the advertisements more Madison Avenue (but for Aquarian concerns, of course). The articles were often less self-consciously utopian and more mainstream. The hippies—after the bewildering hiatus of the seventies—were becoming yuppies, and in large numbers. They were no longer identified with the cultural fringe. They were even, in some senses, establishment in outlook.

Instead of "tuning in, turning on, and dropping out," as psychedelic savant Timothy Leary preached, they are "transforming their consciousness" through nonpsychedelic Americanized mystical practices such as Silva Mind Control, TM, and various consciousness-raising seminars and therapies. Instead of dropping out they are moving up—as doctors, journalists, lawyers, politicians, and educators. *New Age Journal* had to meet the needs of this new New Age readership.

However, the move to mainstream by no means meant conservatism in any sense of the term. You won't find any advertisements for the Conservative Book Club in *New Age Journal*. The sensibilities of the left are still generally in place, if not as consciously articulated. The spirituality of the East and the occult is still assumed but not as often spotlighted. Yet the move toward the mainstream seems to have disenchanted some old-liners who yearn for the good old days of *New Age*.

The April 1990 issue printed a letter lamenting the loss of transparently New Age ideas in *New Age Journal*. Concerning the November/December 1989 issue the letter writer said, "I quickly scanned the table of contents for the latest articles on 'new age' ideas. However, I was deeply disappointed to discover they had all been left out." The writer bemoans the absence of anything "about spirit, God, meditation, states of consciousness, spiritual teachers, yoga, dharma, visions, dreams." The writer complains that he could have just as well picked up *Ladies Home Journal, Popular Mechanics,* or *Psychology Today!* The writer ends by asserting that *New Age Journal* "is getting away from the very things that made your magazine special. Please get back on track; the world needs you."

The disgruntled writer was only partially correct. Even if every article in the magazine lacked cosmic clout, nearly every advertisement would bring us back to the shores of the mystic deep— whether they be for books on channeling, psalmistry, or reincarnation; occult technologies to alter brain states (in record time); subliminal tapes to unleash the sleeping Success within; or any number of other spiritually charged allurements.

But what of the content of recent *New Age* articles?

For the New Age movement to exist as potent cultural force, it must adapt to its surroundings. The age of the mega-gurus is probably over—with the death of Rajneesh burying the phenomena. America, though suffering from spiritual vertigo, is still historically Judeo-Christian and not Eastern in heritage. Explicit appeals to exotic and alien religions are not likely to fare as well as topics of universal concern—such as relationships, career, politics, environment—handled within a generally pantheistic and monistic framework. C. S. Lewis noted that books in which the Christian world view is "latent" can do more to further Christianity than books specifically on Christianity. Just as one might better convince a sceptic of the credibility of Christianity by having him read a noteworthy Christian treatment of a current issue than by assigning an apologetic text, the New Age world view may be more subtly and effectively conveyed through this latent method.

Our disgruntled letter writer needn't despair for long in his search for hard-core, old-line New Age ideas. Any number of magazines—with occultically unabashed names such as *Gnosis, Magical Blend, The Shaman's Drum,* and *Yoga Journal*—are dedicated to the straight stuff of pagan spirituality. In fact, the very issue of *New Age Journal* in which his letter appeared features an article called "Spiritual Revision" that advises dropping any religious beliefs that cause guilt. (So much for original—or subsequent—sin.) There is also an interview with "geologian" Father Thomas Berry, who seems more enthralled with Mother Earth than Father God. Another article called "New Horizons" concerns the spirituality of astronauts who, having had access to ascended vantage points, view the earth as their living Mother. (We should remember Chesterton's quip from *Orthodoxy* that the earth is not our mother but our sister.)

New Age Journal hasn't forgotten its roots. It is simply less blatant and more universal in appeal. (While I was speaking on the New Age movement at a respected Christian liberal arts college in the Midwest, one student informed me that *New Age Journal* could be purchased at the university book store.) And its subscription base is significantly higher than its more overtly spiritual cousins such as *Gnosis.* By mellowing its metaphysics it stands to draw new readers into the New Age fold by offering articles of general interest to sensitive yuppies who have yet to consult channelers, buy cosmic crystals, or visualize world peace. After several issues, though, the spiritually inquisitive could likely become involved in any number of practices, ideas, and movements appearing in *New Age Journal*—from acupuncture to Zen meditation.

At the same time, as our concerned letter writer notes, *New Age Journal* might accommodate to "worldly" trends to the point of losing its uniquely New Age nerve. One's theology can become so latent as to become invisible. What lies ahead for the editorial brain power at *New Age Journal* is likely a carefully executed balancing act between occult overload and pedestrian pandering.

If the brief history of *New Age Journal* is a key to understanding the New Age movement as a whole, we can venture a few observations. Despite its high visibility in recent years, the New Age movement lacks a defined identity. Its flexibility, Taoist aphorisms notwithstanding, could mean its downfall. The branch that bends in the wind will not break. It may instead feebly flap in the breeze and inspire few salutes. Yet despite the deficits of malleability, the New Age heralds the ancient doctrine of human perfectibility, celebrating what Renaissance occultists called "the terrestrial God," a.k.a. anthropos. If pantheism is, as Lewis put it, "the natural bent of the human mind when left to itself," we can expect it to appeal—with varying degrees of success—to fallen god-players through a diversity of forms until the imitated One returns to gather his own and forever scuttle all counterfeits.

21

The Shamanized Jesus

Almost lost amidst the vociferous opposition to the 1988 film *The Last Temptation of Christ* was the fact that the Jesus of the film espouses New Age theology. The movie has Jesus pantheistically proclaiming that "everything is a part of God," a remark that caused *Time* to think of this revised Jesus as "a recent graduate of the Shirley MacLaine school of theology." After picking up some dirt and stones, Jesus says, "This too is my body," signifying the cosmos. Not surprisingly, several New Age thinkers hailed the movie as a challenge to the church to radically rethink the orthodox image of Jesus.

The New Age movement claims Jesus as one of its own. Rather than being exiled to the lore of religious legend or debunked as a messianic pretender, Jesus is favored as an enlightened master who manifested a divine power available to all. He is, according to New Age author John White, "a harbinger of the New Age."[1]

The New Age movement is an eclectic and confusing conglomeration of spiritual seekers who have despaired of finding personal and cosmic satisfaction in either religious orthodoxies or secular materialism. Instead, they have turned to exotic and esoteric sources—increasingly available and mass marketed—

in the hopes of finding what they seek in the unorthodox ambiance of the mystical, magical, and metaphysical. Given these tendencies, the biblical Jesus holds little fascination. Jesus, they think, must be rescued from a parochial orthodoxy that claims he had a monopoly on deity. The issue with New Agers is not whether Jesus is God in human form. They affirm this. The issue is whether Jesus is uniquely God incarnate, or whether we are all God in human form.

The Lost Jesus

The New Age movement has no single view of Jesus, but it offers a family of related views whose common factors can be summarized.

First, the New Age esteems Jesus as a spiritually attuned or evolved being who serves as an example for spiritual discovery and evolutionary advancement. Jesus is referred to in various terms of metaphysical endearment, including Master, Guru, Yogi, Adept, Avator, and Shaman. He is a member of the spiritual hall of fame along with Buddha, Krishna, Lao Tse, and others.

Second, the New Age separates the historical Jesus from the universal and impersonal Christ consciousness. Jesus merely tapped into this cosmic power. New Age philosopher David Spangler, echoing the ancient Gnostics, said that "the Christ is not the province of a single individual."[2] As Joseph Campbell put it in the best-selling *The Power of Myth*: "We are all manifestations of Buddha consciousness, of Christ consciousness, only we don't know it."[3] Christhood comes through self-discovery; we may all become Christs if we harness the universal energy.

Third, the affirmation that Jesus is the supreme and final revelation of God is denied. Although Jesus is respected, he is not "crowned with many crowns" as the one true Lord. Janet Bock complains that "the position that Jesus was the only 'Son of God' . . . is, in effect, a limiting of the power of God, a shackling of divinity to one physical form for all eternity."[4]

Fourth, Jesus' crucifixion, if recognized at all, is not deemed as having any atoning significance. Jesus' suffering on the cross is either rejected as unhistorical or reinterpreted to exclude the idea that he suffered to pay the penalty for sin. Elizabeth Clare Prophet, leader of the Church Universal and Triumphant, stated emphatically that the idea of a blood sacrifice is "an erroneous doctrine," that it is "a remnant of pagan rite long refuted by the word of God."[5]

Fifth, Jesus' resurrection and ascension are routinely denied or spiritualized so as to exclude his unique triumph over sin, death, and Satan. Many others are recognized as "ascended masters." In *The Power of Myth,* Campbell interprets the ascension to mean that Jesus "has gone inward . . . to the place from which all being comes, into the consciousness that is the source of all things, the kingdom of heaven within."[6] Jesus does not ascend to the Father but descends to the divine depths of the collective soul.

Sixth, Jesus' second coming is spiritualized and democratized to include the evolutionary ascent of an awakened humanity. Soli, an "off-planet being" channeled through Neville Rowe, offers this eschatological insight: "You are God, You are, each and every one, part of the Second Coming."[7] The notion that "this same Jesus" (Acts 1:11) who bodily ascended to heaven will himself return in like manner on judgment day is rejected as narrow-minded literalism.

Seventh, the New Age accepts arcane, extrabiblical documents as sources for authentic information about Jesus. Although the Bible is selectively cited, its function is secondary to texts that reveal a different Jesus. Regarding the New Testament either as questionable or unreliable, New Agers often turn to several supposedly historical records of Jesus.

Many believe that Gnostic texts discovered at Nag Hammadi, Egypt, provide a trustworthy record of Jesus as a spiritual catalyst who came to awaken the spark of divinity locked in corporeal confinement. Self-knowledge or *gnosis* is the means of salvation. Many falsely assume that the Gnostic materials, such as the Gospel of Thomas or the Gospel of Peter, are historically trustworthy documents that were rejected by orthodoxy for self-serving reasons.

Another strand of historical revisionism harks back to a book called *The Unknown Life of Jesus Christ,* published in 1894 by a

Russian journalist, Nicholas Notovitch. This book claims to unveil an ancient Tibetan record of Jesus' "lost years" (between ages thirteen and twenty-nine), which he spent studying, teaching, and traveling in the mystic East. This Jesus, called Saint Issa, bears little resemblance to the central figure of the Gospels but serves to synthesize Judaism, Christianity, and Eastern religions into one artificial theological hodgepodge.

Others find the key to Jesus in the ancient Essene community near the Dead Sea. Looking to the Dead Sea Scrolls, they see Jesus as part of a mystical remnant preserved from the fundamentalism of his day. MacLaine puts forth this thesis by saying that "Jesus and the Essenes, with their teachings on love and light and cosmic laws along with the Golden Rule of karma, sound very much like metaphysical seekers in the New Age today."[8]

These esoteric materials are often augmented or eclipsed by revelations originating beyond history. Channelers or mediums receive messages about Jesus from personal spirit beings such as Ramtha (through J. Z. Knight). Others, such as Edgar Cayce and Rudolph Steiner, key into an impersonal, celestial hard drive called the Akashic Records or the Collective Unconscious, to extract Christologies strikingly at odds with Holy Writ. The popular, pseudo-Christian three-volume set *A Course in Miracles* claims to have been dictated by Jesus himself, although it denies doctrines such as original sin, the vicarious atonement of Christ, justification by faith, and a literal heaven and hell.

Eighth, when the Bible is cited with reference to Jesus, an appeal is made to an "esoteric" dimension lost on the esoteric masses of wooden literalists. The Bible must be decoded to discern the secret teaching. So, according to some New Age writers, when Jesus said that John the Baptist was Elijah, he was referring to reincarnation. When he said "the kingdom of heaven is within you," he really meant the divinity of the soul.

The New Age offers to Jesus erroneous endorsements and confused commendations. Jesus is severed from scriptural moorings and anchored in an alien environment glittering with New Age allure. Jesus, the Christ-conscious Master, is our prototype for spiritual discovery and power. Yet he is a Christ without cross or physical resurrection, preaching a gospel without repentance or forgiveness, before an audience of potential equals without sin or shame who are in no peril of perdition.

A Question of Documents

How, then, can we affirm that Jesus Christ has "the name that is above every name" (Phil. 2:9) in the face of a growing number who deny his supremacy while confessing his greatness?

The accusation that the Christ of Christianity "doesn't work" has some sting to it. American Christianity too often fails to demonstrate the living reality of Jesus through sound teaching, clear thinking, moral courage, and compassion. Many New Agers complain that the church has failed them. Perhaps our vision of the real Jesus has faded and we are content with status-quo religion instead of discipleship under the cross of Christ.

While we must insist with Os Guinness that "Christianity isn't true because it works, it works because it's true," we should also remember what Francis Schaeffer called "the final apologetic": Jesus himself said that the world would judge the truth of Jesus by the love his followers manifest (John 13:34–35; 17:21). Given the indispensable foundation of ethical integrity, theological and historical arguments can be marshaled to establish the biblical Jesus as authentic and to unmask the New Age impostor.

First, we should outline a response to criticisms that the biblical sources themselves are unreliable or inferior to other documents about Jesus. As it happens, the standard arguments for the trustworthiness of the New Testament are often not so much rejected as ignored in New Age circles.

New Agers routinely undervalue the New Testament because of its antiquity, its manner of compilation, and the number of translations and editions. This criticism can be defused by emphasizing that the New Testament is the best attested collection of ancient literature with regard to the number and quality of manuscripts. Some 5,366 partial or complete Greek manuscripts have been recovered, dating as far back as the end of the first century. The large number of manuscripts gives scholars a rich resource for reconstructing the original text.

Beyond this, the date of the original writings is close to the events described—in most cases, not more than a generation removed. This is more than can be said for most ancient literature. Those who wrote the documents were also in a good position to ascertain the truth of their research, being either eyewitnesses or privy to eyewitnesses.

Concerning the canonization of the New Testament, the New Age contends that it was the product of a fourth-century theological elite that excluded legitimate sources for purely political reasons. As intriguing as this scenario may be, it does not bear historical scrutiny. The documents were not given authority as much as they were recognized as already functioning in the churches with authority. Furthermore, books not included in the canon were excluded for specific reasons, such as authorship, doctrine, and use in the church.

In light of this evidence, the burden of proof lies on any other purported record of the life of Jesus. Upon inspection, these revisionist documents fall by the historical wayside.

The Gnostic texts are second-century creations giving heretical reflections on an already existing orthodox view of Jesus. The New Testament is far better attested than Gnostic texts. None of the Nag Hammadi text, for instance, takes the form of an actual gospel. Rather, they are largely metaphysical discourses.

The document claiming to reveal "the lost years of Jesus" spent in India, Persia, and elsewhere was soundly refuted shortly after its publication by noted Orientalist F. Max Muller and others. Despite continued interest in *The Unknown Life of Jesus Christ,* the original manuscript has never been available for scholarly study, and there is no adequate verification of its existence. Surely it is better to have 5,366 Greek manuscripts in the hand than (at most) one exotic manuscript lost in the Tibetan bush.

Claims that Jesus was a New Ager by virtue of being an Essene mystic are refuted on two grounds. First, the Essenes were militantly monotheistic Jews who, despite sectarian idiosyncrasies, affirmed human sinfulness, hell, and a predestinating, personal God—hardly New Age theology! Second, despite some similarity between Jesus' teachings and the Essenes' (due largely to their common reverence for the Old Testament), there is a deep rift between them concerning asceticism, ethics, salvation, and other issues. Jesus was no Essene, and the Essenes were not New Agers.

As to channeled material, we can only ask why someone would give credence to revelations with no historical verification over document connected with factual history, especially when these channeled sources deny the central tenets of what Christians have affirmed for two thousand years.

Confronting Exclusivity

Having argued for the source of authority about Jesus, it is critical to emphasize the exclusivity of the biblical Jesus. In an age of religious relativism, New Agers resist affirmations of absolute truth and authority. Yet many are ignorant of the actual claims of Jesus in the Gospels and the claims made about him in the rest of Scripture.

In John 3:16, Jesus speaks of himself as God's "one and only Son." No other shares that status. Peter preached this Jesus, announcing: "Salvation is found in no one else, for there is no other name under heaven given to men by which we must be saved" (Acts 4:12). This leaves no room for qualification.

Another resounding anthem of exclusivity is found in John 14:6, where Jesus says, "I am the way and the truth and the life. No one comes to the Father except through me." Yet some claim that Jesus is not speaking of himself as the way, but of the impersonal "I Am Presence" in us all! Such interpretive gymnastics, often performed by New Agers, are the result of what James Sire calls "world-view confusion": an entirely alien philosophy (pantheism) superimposed on the biblical message. These esoteric detours around Jesus can be countered by a good dose of common sense. If nothing stated in the text indicates the esoteric meaning, what possible grounds can be given to support the interpretation—besides wishful thinking?

Many other passages single out Jesus as unique and supreme and should be part of our apologetic and evangelistic repertoire. But the assertion of Jesus as *the* way" must be augmented by

argument. Jesus' exclusive claims were backed up by impecca-
ble credentials.

Most people involved in the New Age grant the legitimacy of a
"paranormal" dimension beyond the visible that can affect the
natural realm. They are not skeptics about the supernatural. If
anything, they tend to be credulous. If we emphasize Jesus as a
man of miracles who restored the blind, deaf, dumb, and leprous;
cast out demons with a word; commanded the elements themselves; summoned Lazarus from the grave; and himself rose from
the dead, we may catch their interest and draw them deeper into
the gospel record.

The sheer number, power, and attestation of Jesus' miracles
put him in a category by himself; but the miracles alone are not
sufficient to establish Jesus as Lord. As seventeenth-century apologist Thomas Glanville put it: "'Tis not the doing of wonderful
things that is the only evidence that the holy Jesus was from God
. . . but the conjunction of other circumstances. The holiness of
his life, the reasonableness of his religion, and the excellency of
his designs, added credit to his works and strengthened the great
conclusion, that he could be no other than the Son of God."[9]

This "conjunction of other circumstances" includes Jesus' un-
rivaled authority as a teacher; the certainty of his words regarding his mission, his identity, and the need for human response;
his fulfillment of prophecy; and his love toward those he came
to rescue. These factors show Jesus as a man of integrity and compassion as well as a man of power. He had the power to save the
lost whom he loved.

It is imperative to see Jesus' compassion in light of his assessment of human nature. In the New Age, humans are divine in
essence, if not in experience. Jesus, on the contrary, taught the
"humanity of humanity" and the reality of a ruined race "east of
Eden." Jesus' love cannot be reduced to the desire to see ignorant
deities discover their identity and so share in his Christhood. He
catalogued thirteen items of infamy—such as adultery, greed,
impurity—as "coming from within" and making a person unclean
(Mark 7:21–23). Where the New Age sees a sleeping god, Jesus finds
a tempest of transgression.

Jesus presented himself as the answer to the moral problem of humanity. "The Son of Man did not come to be served, but to serve, and to give his life as a ransom for many" (Mark 10:45). The language of vicarious atonement—so antithetical to New Age self-salvation—is often on Jesus' lips. Speaking of his death, Jesus said, "This is my blood of the covenant, which is poured out for many for the forgiveness of sins" (Matt. 26:27).

The crucifixion, when properly explained, can be a magnet for New Age interest for one stark reason. New Age theology reduces God to an impersonal, amoral force. Humans may partake of the divine essence, but the ultimate reality is inhuman. The Great Void makes no friends and sheds no blood.

But as humans made in God's image, we yearn for loving relationships. The cross expresses a personal God's sacrificial love toward us. God's holiness demands that a price be paid for sin; his love extends a sinless sacrifice for sinners. As Paul said, "While we were still sinners, Christ died for us" (Rom. 5:8). What greater demonstration of love can be imagined? What greater demonstration of power than the resurrection of this Jesus from the dead (Rom. 1:4)?

Yet an appreciation of this love presupposes an awareness of sin. Jesus' love is nothing if not understood as a love for sinners. Blaise Pascal elucidated the balance to be found in Jesus alone: "The Incarnation shows man the greatness of his wretchedness by the greatness of the remedy required."[10]

The gospel is not a spiritual pick-me-up, but an objective claim on every individual. Although Jesus singled himself out of the spiritual crowd through his exclusive claims to divinity and unmatched credentials, he issues an inclusive invitation: "Come to me, all you who are weary and burdened, and I will give you rest" (Matt. 11:28). Christ promises and provides rest from the futile human quest for Christhood that animates New Age spirituality. We may, by his grace, become his friends, but never his peers.[11]

22

Myth and the Power of Joseph Campbell

The surprise best-seller of the summer of 1987 was *The Closing of the American Mind* by Allan Bloom. The surprise best-seller of the summer of 1988 was *The Power of Myth* by Joseph Campbell. Bloom, a philosophy professor, laments the erosion of the rational mind so esteemed in the classical and enlightenment traditions. His jeremiad is aimed at the academic establishment and a popular culture lost in relativism, subjectivism, and low-brow infatuations. Campbell, a literature professor, laments the erosion of the mythic imagination so venerated throughout the millennia by prophets, shamans, and mystics alike. His concern is aimed at those who have suppressed or opposed a mythic understanding of reality in exchange for a hollow rationalism or literalistic religion.

Bloom champions the logos, Campbell the mythos. Bloom points us toward Plato and Rousseau while Campbell waxes lyrical about Hindu cosmology and aboriginal shamanic rites. Bloom, appropriately enough, discourses in academic manner (sans footnotes), producing a thick, ponderous tome, although one not lacking in vitality and passion. Campbell's work takes the shape of a warm, wide-ranging, engaging dialogue with veteran journalist Bill Moyers and is richly illustrated with examples from world mythology and religion.

The Power of Myth is drawn from a series of interviews done in 1985 and 1986 and first shown on public television in 1988, about six months after Campbell's death. The work serves as a summing up of Campbell's thought as a long-time professor at Sarah Lawrence College and a prolific writer on mythology and literature. The eight chapters range over such subjects as the role of mythology in the modern world, the journey inward, the hero's adventure, and tales of love and marriage.

The popularity of both Bloom and Campbell alerts us to the thirst for and importance of metaphysics. Both authors find Western culture fragmented and lacking ultimate foundations. Bloom seldom refers to deity, yet everywhere engages ultimate issues of the good, the true, and the beautiful. Assorted deities crowd in on nearly every page of Campbell's work.

Campbell's charm lies in an encyclopedic grasp of world mythology and religion, winningly presented with a masterful storytelling ability (especially evident on the television series). Campbell was a man who, in his own words, "followed his bliss," and his enthusiasm for the subject matter is evident in both book and series.

The Meaning of Myth

For Campbell, the "power of myth" is the power of metaphor and poetry to capture the imaginations of individuals and societies. Myth supplies a sense of meaning and direction that transcends mundane existence while giving it significance. It has four functions (p. 31). The *mystical* function discloses the world of mystery and awe, making the universe "a holy picture." The *cosmological* function concerns science and the constitution of the universe. The *sociological* function "supports and validates a certain social order." Everyone must try to relate to the *pedagogic* function, which tells us "how to live a human lifetime under any circumstances." America, he believes, has lost its collective ethos and must return to a mythic understanding of life "to bring us into a level of consciousness that is spiritual" (p. 14).

Campbell heralds the benefits of myths, defending them as literally false but metaphorically true for the broad range of human experience. But certain myths are, at least in part, to be rejected as "out of date," particularly the personal lawgiver God of Jews and Christians. Biblical cosmology, he thinks, does not "accord with our concept of either the universe or of the dignity of men. It belongs entirely somewhere else" (p. 31).

Campbell's own mythic commitment is to the "transtheological" notion of an "undefinable, inconceivable mystery, thought of as a power, that is the source and end supporting ground of all life and being." He rejects the term *pantheism* because it may retain a residue of the personal God of theism. Campbell repeatedly hammers home this notion of an ineffable ground of reality: "God is beyond all names and forms. Meister Eckhart said that the ultimate and highest leave taking is leaving God for God, leaving our notion of God for an experience of that which transcends all notions" (p. 49). He pursues this further by noting that "God . . . is beyond pairs of opposites," and, waxing Kantian, "the thing in itself is no thing. It transcends thingness" (p. 49).

Despite the epistemological veto on knowing anything transcendent, Campbell draws on Jung's theory of a collective unconscious to help explain the common ideas or archetypes that reoccur in the mythologies of divergent cultures worldwide. "All over the world and at different times of human history, these archetypes or elementary ideas have appeared in different costumes. The differences in the costumes are the results of environment and historical conditions" (pp. 51, 52).

But not all archetypes are created equal. Campbell singles out the Christian notion of sin as especially pernicious because it stifles human potential. If you confess your sins you make yourself a sinner; if you confess your greatness you make yourself great. The "idea of sin puts you in a servile position throughout your life" (p. 56). He later redefines sin as a lack of knowledge, not as an ethical transgression: "Sin is simply a limiting factor that limits your consciousness and fixes it in an inappropriate condition" (p. 57).

It seems, to steal a phrase from Swami Vivekananda, that the only sin is to call someone a sinner. Campbell believes our challenge is to say, "I know the center, and I know that good and evil are simply temporal aberrations and that, in God's view, there is no difference" (p. 66). In fact, "in God's view," you are "God, not in your ego, but in your deepest being, where you are at one with the nondual transcendent" (p. 211).

The thematic richness of this work could occupy several reviewers, each focusing on different aspects of Campbell's book—anthropological, literary, historical, and sociological. Shunning this polymathic program, I will consider some of the philosophical, religious, and societal issues generated by Campbell's perspective.

Transcendental Mystery

A salient feature of Campbell's world view is a pronounced inconsistency that, unless flushed out, may remain under the wraps of his winsomeness.

According to Campbell, myth opens us to the realm of transcendental mystery where awe and inspiration energize and permeate our beings. But given Campbell's epistemological veto of any cognitive knowledge of the transcendent, we can say nothing concrete of it. It is beyond concepts, names, and thought. It is metaphysically mute. Campbell wants to vindicate myths as existentially compelling by saying that they are not to be taken concretely, but metaphorically. Yet even metaphors are incorrigibly conceptual; poetry says something. Propositions are pesky things. They are difficult to fumigate. The Hindu myth of a blood-soaked, skull-adorned Mother Kali destroying the world carries with it the nonmetaphorical meaning that God is as much Destroyer as Creator. That's the theology of it, even when taken as myth and not history.

Campbell himself enthusiastically disregards his epistemological veto by issuing many conceptual statements about that which (supposedly) transcends concepts entirely. Campbell affirms that the ground of all forms is impersonal not personal. This assumes definite knowledge of the ontology of divinity. He sees this impersonal source of all being as beyond ethical categories, so we must say yes to all of life, no matter how degraded. Yet this too assumes definite knowledge of the character of the transcendent as amoral, not moral. The transcendent is also "nondual" as opposed to dual or triune. All myths, he affirms, point to an invisible world beyond the world of visible form. Further, "we are all manifestations of the Buddha consciousness or the Christ consciousness, only we don't know it" (p. 57). (We are, then, not conscious of our divine consciousness.) Again, specific propositions are affirmed, and in quite nonmetaphorical language. Campbell's "transcendental silence" has a habit of speaking out on metaphysics. The explicit epistemological veto is overridden by an implicit theology that welcomes pantheism and filters out theism. Despite his statement that "the person who thinks he has found the ultimate truth is wrong" (p. 55), Campbell asserts the ultimate truth of an impersonal and amoral divinity.

Campbell marshals no arguments as to why we should reckon the transcendent as impersonal. The closest he comes is in discussing an encounter with a Roman Catholic priest, in which the priest asked him if he believed in a personal God, thus supposedly granting the possibility of an impersonal God. The anecdote is no argument. The priest was simply being wise in defining a theological issue; he was not necessarily granting the plausibility of an impersonal God by granting that the idea has some currency.

Campbell himself rejects the idea of God as "Absolutely Other" because, he says, we can have no relationship with that in which we do not participate. Yet how we, as personal and morally responsible beings, can conceptualize or experience a religious relationship with an impersonal and amoral ground of the universe is less than clear.

Literalism on Trial

Campbell is ever at odds with a religious literalism that reifies mythic themes into concrete, historical facts. He refers to the biblical creation story that teaches an actual beginning of the universe as "artificialism" and chides Bill Moyers for considering the resurrection of Christ in historical terms. He says this historical view "is a mistake in reading the symbol"; it is to read "the words in terms of prose instead of in terms of poetry" and to read "the metaphor in terms of denotation instead of the connotation" (p. 57). In fact, Jesus' ascension into heaven, metaphorically interpreted, means that "he has gone inward—not into outer space but into inner space, to the place from which all beings come, into the consciousness that is the source of all things, the kingdom of heaven within" (p. 56).

Given this method of interpretation, Campbell is much happier with post-Christian Gnosticism than orthodoxy. He quotes favorably from a passage in The Gospel of Thomas where Jesus teaches that "he who drinks from my mouth will become as I am," and properly notes that "this is blasphemy in the normal way of Christian thinking" (p. 57).

Campbell's mythic hermeneutic has the appearance of profundity. He uses it profitably to interpret a vast amount of mythological literature. He likens mistaking a metaphor for its reference to eating a menu instead of the meal. Yet when Campbell addresses biblical materials, such as the Gospels or Acts, which were written as history—not poetry or visionary literature—his metaphoric interpretation is forced at best. Certainly, the significance of the ascension of Christ for Christian theology is not exhausted by spatial location, yet the physical reference is intrinsic to the significance that Christ is not bound to earth. He has ascended to the right hand of the Father where he now reigns. Campbell may not believe this to be literally true, but the apostles did and the church still does. A more judicious reading would note that a miraculous truth claim is being made, either to be accepted or rejected—not reinterpreted by a mythical hermeneutic. Instead of eating the menu, Campbell misreads it and fancies a meal never mentioned.

The classic Christian text on the historicity of the resurrection of Christ is Paul's insistence to the Corinthian church that if Christ be not raised Christian faith is in vain. Moreover, if the resurrection is factually false, apostolic preaching is futile and misrepresents God, Christians are left in their sin, departed Christians have perished, and Christians are of all people most pitiful. Paul had no mere mythic symbol in mind here. Neither would the early Christians have died martyrs' deaths for metaphors. The apostle Peter, in his second epistle, went so far as to say that "we did not follow cleverly invented stories when we told you about the power and coming of our Lord Jesus Christ, but we were eyewitnesses of his majesty" (1:16).

Campbell is pleased with diverse mythic expressions so long as they refer only to the unknowable transcendent. But he rejects the concept of a fallen creation in need of external redemption made known through a historically grounded revelation from a *personal* God. He expresses amazement at the Hebraic commandment "Thou shalt have no other gods before me." Such militant monotheism curtails the mythic imagination. Campbell chokes on the hard historicity of Christianity, and is not comfortable until he recasts it in metaphorical terms.

Myth Become Fact

Yet orthodox Christianity need not jettison uncritically Campbell's mythic concerns. Christian writers like C. S. Lewis have argued that the world's mythologies present a dim imitation of the redemption made historical through Christ. Mythologies worldwide speak of lost innocence, cosmic conflict, and redemption. In this sense the mythic dimension can be seen as part of general revelation, not in itself salvific, but as pointing beyond itself to what Lewis called "myth become fact," the incarnation itself:

> The heart of Christianity is a myth which is also a fact. The old myth of the dying God, without ceasing to be myth, comes down from the heaven of legend and imagination to the earth of history. It happens—at a particular date, in a particular place, followed by debatable historical consequences. We pass from a Balder or an Osiris, dying nobody knows when or where, to an historical Person crucified (it is all in order) under Pontius Pilate.[1]

Campbell largely dismisses the historicity of Christianity by saying that we don't know much about Jesus, given we only have "four contradictory texts that purport to tell us what he said and did" (p. 211). He adds that, in spite of these supposed contradictions, we know "approximately what Jesus said" (p. 211). If Campbell would have taken seriously the idea of a basic historical record of Jesus' words, he might have been less inclined to recast Christianity in mythic terms. The wealth of historical material provided by the Gospels, while not without some complexities, reveals a concern for historical accuracy and integrity, particularly Luke's prologue which claims to present an orderly account based on careful investigation.

Campbell quotes Jesus as saying, "No one gets to the Father but by me" (from John's Gospel), but in the same breath skips to the Hindu goddess Kali as an equally appropriate metaphor for God, the transcendent unknown (p. 20). Yet if the historical record of Jesus is even "approximately" accurate we can't have it both ways. The goddess Kali, never meant to be viewed as a historical embodiment of God, is smeared with the human blood of those she has murdered and whose skulls she wears around her neck. Christ, worshiped as the historical incarnation, sheds his own blood for others at Golgotha, the place of the skull. Any reduction of Christ to Kali is simply oblivious to the obvious. Can the "transcendent unknown" justify contradictory claims concerning ultimate reality? If so, where does that leave logic?

Mythology and Public Life

How would Campbell's mythic world view describe public life? Campbell expresses concern that hollow rationalism and literalistic religion are inadequate to meet modern needs. Although he doesn't develop a social philosophy, we can infer some clues.

First, Campbell's ethical foundations and evaluations remain unrelated to any enduring moral order. He states "the final secret of myth [is] to teach you how to penetrate the labyrinth of life in such a way that spiritual values come through" (p. 115). The sociological function of myth is to validate a given social order. Yet these spiritual values are relative to various cultures and historical epochs. Myths are all "true" but some must be adapted to modern needs and realities. Campbell deems unecological the Christian cosmology of the earth as separate from God, and instead opts for a not yet fully developed "planetary mythology" that resacralizes the universe along Buddhist lines. He also speaks out strongly against the white man's abuse of the Indians, their animals, and their land, and calls this "a sacramental violation" (p. 78).

Given Campbell's cosmic amoralism—God as beyond morality—it remains to be seen how any judgment or mythical imperative could be ethically binding or normative. The Good is not based on God's unchanging moral character as a personal being; it is not knowable through God's self-disclosure. The transcendent is ineffable and therefore morally mute as well as metaphysically mute. Any mythic recommendation for individuals or society is simply an inexplicable archetypal upsurge of the ultimately unknown and unknowable. Campbell's advocacy of a "planetary mythology" is mere vision with no vindication of its value.

Second, Campbell's ethics are further eroded by a tendency toward monism, so often tied to pantheism. In explaining the heroic deed of a policeman to save a man attempting suicide, Campbell invokes Schopenhauer's notion that "you and the other are one, that you are two aspects of the one life, and that your apparent separateness is but an effect of the way we experience forms under the conditions of space and time. Our true reality is in our identity and unity with all life" (p. 110). Any act of human sacrifice is really reducible to cosmic selfism. In helping "others" we are really helping ourselves. All altruism ends as esoteric egotism. Elsewhere Moyers paraphrases Campbell by adapting a command of Jesus: "love thy neighbor as thyself because thy neighbor is thyself" (p. 111).

As G. K. Chesterton put it in *Orthodoxy*, this is not a call to love our neighbors; it is a call to be our neighbors, and it makes the universe one enormously selfish person (actually not even a person if the ultimate reality is impersonal). If the subject-object distinction is not ultimately real the very idea of self-giving or self-sacrifice must be sacrificed on the monistic altar. Any action could be justified in terms of cosmic selfism. If all is one, how could we violate others' rights? Social ethics would be rendered as sociological solitaire.

Third, the monistic model is at odds with Campbell's praise for the West's positive emphasis on the individual's worth and freedom. Individualism (in the positive sense of the dignity of individuals) can be praised only if one adopts a (nonmonistic) ontology of actual, singular entities (humans and otherwise) and a corresponding ethic that respects the right of individual expression. Individualism historically has not fared well in nations such as India where monism monitors morality.

Fourth, although Campbell has many harsh words for Christian theism, which has served as the foundation for so many Western individual liberties, he reserves judgment on extreme tribal practices such as head-hunting and initiations requiring sexual profligacy and even human sacrifice. He sees these ritual acts simply as enacted mythologies vital to cultural life.

Fifth, in a telltale passage, Campbell contrasts the ancient religion of the Goddess with that of the Bible: "You get a totally different way of living according to whether your myth presents nature as fallen or whether nature is in itself a manifestation of divinity, and the spirit is the revelation of the divinity that is inherent in nature" (p. 99). Campbell clearly chooses the latter and says that "one of the glorious things about Goddess religions is that "the world is the body of the Goddess, divine in itself, and divinity isn't ruling over a fallen nature." This, in fact, seems to be Campbell's model for society: a social order uninhibited by any supernatural authority or by any recognition of inexorable human fallibility and moral aberration.

Unfallen Founders?

Campbell offers the United States as an example of a social order that does not assume the fall. He paints the founders as appealing to pure reason unhindered by any innate human corruption. "For these men, there is no special revelation anywhere,

and none is needed, because the mind of man cleared of its fal-
libilities is sufficiently capable of the knowledge of God" (p. 25).

Now, of course, for Campbell there is no real knowledge of the
unknown transcendent, but he does seem to endorse the
founders' purported pronouncements. No one debates the deis-
tic impetus present in some of the founders, but to make the blan-
ket statement that they all rejected both human fallenness and
special revelation is historically unfounded. One need only read
the *Federalist Papers* to find a judicious understanding of human
limitation and its bearing on civil governance. The very notion
of the division of powers assumes that since humans tend to
abuse power, governmental administration should be balanced
in three separate branches. As *Federalist 51* (written by Madison)
puts it, "If men were angels, no government would be necessary.
If angels were to govern men, neither external nor internal con-
trols on government would be necessary." And neither were
explicit appeals to special revelation lacking in the writing and
oratory of many of the founders. The Bible was too much a part
of the nation's ethical discourse and historical memory to be so
shunned.

Unlike the historical American ideal, Campbell's mythic world
view allows for no appeal to "inalienable rights" granted to all by
their creator. That would be too literalistic and absolutistic. Nor
could there be violations of human dignity because we have no
law above the sociologically functioning mythologies that inspire
social order. Instead of a Law above human law we simply have
the ineffable—in the collective unconsciousness—below the
mythological manifestations.

It might appear at first blush that Campbell's mythic permissiveness (no one mythic understanding is ultimately true) would
serve as a solid platform for pluralism. At one point Campbell
says that mythologies are like individual software; if yours works,
don't change it. But the classical liberal—not the modern, relativistic liberal—understanding of pluralism is deeper and wider.
It assumes truth has nothing to fear from a plurality of perspectives; it can compete with and triumph over error in "the marketplace of ideas" by virtue of its own merit. Western liberty of
expression is premised on the right to be right and the right to be

wrong and be proven wrong through dialogue, debate, and discussion. Campbell's mythic pluralism assumes no truth to be discovered, debated, or discussed. The merit of any mythology is not its objective veracity but its subjective pull and social power. Mythic pluralism endorses a relativism that ignores the possibility of uncovering the absolute, the universal or the objective. If the software works, keep it—just so long as you delete any religious literalisms.

Furthermore, no appeal to any higher moral authority is possible for Campbell. The most powerful and commanding mythology of the twentieth century was Marxist-Leninism, with its "fall" of primordial preprivate property paradise into acquisitiveness, dialectical providence, and redemption through revolution. Does Campbell have any basis for judging this mythology false and evil? What's wrong with the software?

What's Left Untried?

Campbell, like Bloom, has diagnosed the modern malady of rootlessness and superficiality. We lack a unified ethos. He, like Bloom, redirects our attention to the ultimate concerns beyond thoughtless diversions. And the book-buying public is responding. Yet just as Bloom's philosophical absolutes remain unrooted in any transcendent and personal realm (the Good as God's character and command), so does Campbell reject the personal Creator God of the monotheistic traditions. But instead of Bloom's natural law, Campbell champions an ineffable, amoral, and impersonal deity.

Given the surprising popularity of both books, I think Campbell's mythic vision will dominate in days ahead. Bloom is tough-minded, demanding logical rigor and analysis, and he rightly rejects relativism. Campbell is highly articulate, but appeals more to the subjective imagination than to the demands of reason. The mythic world of innumerable gods and goddesses of one's own choosing has greater psychological pull than Bloom's holy of holies, the elite university shorn of any superstitious attachments, mythic or otherwise.

Campbell may not have countenanced it, but it may befall him to become a posthumous prophet for New Age sentiments. Although more of an academic than a popularizer, Campbell's essential world view is in basic agreement with that of New Age celebrities like Shirley MacLaine, Werner Erhard, and John Denver: All is one, god is an impersonal and amoral force in which we participate; supernatural revelation and redemption are not needed. Campbell's wide erudition and sophisticated manner may attract those who are less impressed by the metaphysical glitz of MacLaine or the rank superstition of "crystal consciousness" or the cosmic hype of the "Harmonic Convergence."

Campbell is correct: myth in its various functions is potent and pervasive. Human beings needs a comprehensive world view capable of undergirding and integrating individual and social values, engaging the imagination, activating the intellect, and energizing the will. Yet it must also be true. Campbell abandoned what he confessed he could not understand—"Thou shalt have no other gods before me"—and affirmed gods many and lords many. One can only hope his readers will harken to the words of another quite conversant with the power of myth, Chesterton, who said, "The Christian ideal has not been tried and found wanting. It has been found difficult and left untried."[2]

23

Al Gore in the Balance

Vice President Albert Gore's ambitious four-hundred-page best-selling opus, *Earth in the Balance: Ecology and the Human Spirit*,[1] aspires to be no less than an ecological tour de force. This expansive and earnest volume combines scientific analysis, political policy, autobiography, intellectual history, and even a theology of the environment—all presented with the fervor of a conscience-bound activist striving to awaken a sleeping populace to the approaching ecological apocalypse of global warming, ozone depletion, soil erosion, and a host of other environmental ills unrecognized by those who oppose his views.

Because of its encyclopedic aims, *Earth in the Balance* is difficult to review adequately. Instead of delving extensively into controversies over the veracity of Gore's ecological vision, I will focus on the relationship of several roles he attempts to fulfill simultaneously: the politician, the environmentalist, and the self-confessed Baptist.

Gore the Politician

Richard John Neuhaus has sagaciously observed that truth and power are often at odds, and this tension is particularly evident in politics. The temptation is to use information as a manipulative means to a political end, rather than to advance truth as the end in itself. "Since democracy is a raucous enterprise," Neuhaus warns, "we must be prepared for impassioned oversimplifications by which partisans attempt to mobilize their several constituencies. . . . There is an inescapable tension between truth and power, and the mark of moral stature in an activist is that she acknowledges the tension."[2] This maxim makes for a sturdy standard by which to evaluate Vice President Gore—and ourselves.

Although *Time* claims that Gore broke political tradition and wrote this book himself (no doubt with the help of a research staff),[3] it nevertheless sometimes reads like an extended campaign advertisement. The book was published before Gore was officially selected as Bill Clinton's running mate, but Gore is a long-time politician with established ambitions for high office. This probably accounts for the tendency of *Earth in the Balance* to lapse into a somewhat self-serving autobiographical style and a polemical stance against the Bush administration. Gore portrays himself as a globe-trotting ecological hero who investigates environmental issues firsthand.

Gore the Environmentalist

These narratives are not incidental to Gore's case. He has made environmental issues a key theme in his elected service and seems to be genuinely concerned about them. Nevertheless, his travelogues sometimes take the place of detailed argumentation and documentation. And in this we must question Gore's credibility as an environmentalist. He refers often to testimonies before his Senate subcommittees and anecdotal material gleaned from conversations with assorted natives, scientists, and other folk. *Earth in the Balance* is unadorned by a single supporting footnote. Instead we must be content with a bibliography that includes two PBS television programs and a section of narrated notes that refer, often only generally, to sources for Gore's conclusions. Given the radicality of Gore's assessment and agenda—he says "we must all become partners in a bold effort to change the very foundation of our civilization" (p. 14)—a better academic foundation would have been appreciated. Oversimplifications serve an agenda all too easily when the quest for political power overwhelms a respect for truth.

Despite a lack of scholarly documentation, Gore's treatments of global warming, ozone depletion, and various pollution problems tend to be, prima facie, clearly stated and plausibly argued. He distinguishes between ecological problems that are local, regional, and strategic. Local and regional problems do not have global consequences and are more easily correctable than are strategic problems, which involve global systems such as the atmosphere and the oceans. Gore is especially concerned that increased carbon dioxide emissions—largely caused by factors deeply rooted in industrial societies, such as fossil fuels—will eventuate in a gradual warming of the earth's environment. This, in turn, will cause the polar ice caps to melt, which would flood coastal cities, trigger crippling droughts, unleash hurricanes, and cause all manner of other ills. Similarly, ozone depletion would weaken the atmosphere's ability to screen out harmful cancer-causing ultraviolet rays.

In these and other issues Gore's analysis is not indefensible. Many present trends of industrialized societies, if unchecked, could lead to deleterious consequences of global proportions. Instead of rejecting or accepting Gore's assessment for partisan reasons, we should instead investigate the matter carefully—more carefully than Gore does in his book. Because of his passion for this issue and his political ambitions, Gore often sweeps opposing views under the intellectual rug by using at least three different strategies.

Consider global warming. According to Gore, only a small fraction of the scientific community disputes the severity of the situation. But the debate over global warming and the dreaded "greenhouse effect" is hotter than Gore admits. The scientific community is seriously divided as to whether or not global warming is occurring, what causes the warming if it is occurring, what the rate of temperature increase will be if it is occurring, and whether or not a warming trend will be, on balance, better or worse for the planet. A recent Gallup poll reported that 53 percent of scientists actively involved in global climate research do not believe that global warming has occurred; 30 percent say they aren't sure; and only 17 percent affirm that global warming has begun. Even a poll commissioned by Greenpeace, a radical environmentalist group, found that 47 percent of climatologists don't think a runaway greenhouse effect is immanent; 36 percent said it is possible; and only 13 percent said it is probable.[4] But according to this confident politician, only an insignificant minority of "skeptics" disagree with his dire scenario. This is the "avoid the opposition" strategy: Gore assumes there aren't enough credible and unbiased opponents for their views to be taken seriously. Yet Roger Revelle, Gore's mentor at Harvard who is cited approvingly in *Earth in the Balance,* has said, "The scientific base for greenhouse warming is too uncertain to justify drastic action at this time. There is little risk in delaying policy responses."[5]

Second, Gore says that the problems are so momentous that we must stop debating the issue and start taking decisive action. This is the "paralysis of analysis" strategy: Forget about the controversy! We must save the planet! But this response begs the critical questions. Action is not needed if there is no crisis to avert. We don't perform major surgery on the chance that something might be wrong. We need compelling evidence.

But Gore's "global Marshall Plan" is heady stuff. Fueled by the conviction that the salvation of the global environment should be humankind's one overriding ethical principle, Gore advances admittedly radical proposals requiring extensive federal intervention through new taxation, regulations, and massive monetary and technological aid to Third World countries. Critics have considered these proposals rather Draconian, especially in light of the less than overwhelming evidence for some of Gore's key concerns such as global warming.

Concerning Gore's proposal to cap carbon dioxide emissions in the United States by 20 percent of the 1990 levels, Ronald Bailey comments that a U.S. Department of Energy study concluded that this "would require a $500 per-ton carbon tax. Such measures would cost $95 billion per year and reduce U.S. economic growth rates by 1.4 percent."[6]

Third, those who disagree with Gore are often portrayed as tainted by special economic interests, short-sightedness, or blinding political ideology. These egregious elements are not alien in a fallen race, but Gore often invokes them prematurely to "poison the well": these people can't be right because of their corrupt orientations. Poisoning the well is both bad ecology and bad argumentation. Arguments must stand or fall on their rational merits. We may want to explain someone's actions by appealing to bad motives but we cannot refute opposing arguments with such a strategy.

Yet even if Gore is off target in much of his dire analysis of planetary woes, he rightfully highlights ecological imbalances that should be addressed, such as deforestation (especially in Third-World countries), toxic waste, and the need for recycling. Gore refers to concrete examples of environmental abuse that have been confronted by informed and effective activists. This should stir our conscience even if it fails to convert us wholly to his cause.

Gore and Christianity

But what of Gore the self-confessed Christian, a Southern Baptist by denomination and reputed to be a consistent church attender? How does he integrate his ecological and political mission with his Christian faith?

Near the end of *Earth in the Balance,* Gore offers something of a testimony, or at least a confession of faith. General references to the deity are not uncommon on the lips of politicians, but Gore's comments are worth quoting. After speaking of the need for faith in the face of ecological crisis, Gore explains what he means: "My own faith is rooted in the unshakable belief in God as creator and sustainer, a deeply personal interpretation of and relationship with Christ, and an awareness of a constant and holy spiritual presence in all people, all life, and all things" (p. 368). Although this confession remains somewhat vague—what is the "deeply personal interpretation of Christ"?—Gore eclipses the usual theological platitudes. For this reason, his work invites a theological critique.

Gore should be credited with the savvy to address the spiritual dimension of the ecological issue. In the chapter "The Environmentalism of the Spirit" he develops a theology of the environment. Gore begins well by grounding environmental stewardship in the doctrine of creation. The universe belongs to God and should therefore be treated with respect. Yet when Gore says "creation" it is not entirely clear what this implies for him. Throughout the book, Gore accepts macro-evolutionary theory without batting a sceptical eyelash and posits global climatic changes as essential to human evolution. He also relies on the noted atheistic astronomer and pop scientist, Carl Sagan, for some speculative evolutionary views of the development of the human brain.[7]

So it seems that Gore is a theistic evolutionist: God created the raw materials that evolved through natural processes over eons of time. He never specifies whether or not "creation" means creation ex nihilo or some other kind of origination such as creation ex deo, which means that the cosmos is an emanation or externalization of God's essence. The latter view is either pantheistic or panentheistic; it is unbiblical because it denies the essential metaphysical distinction between Creator and creation.[8] But Gore doesn't define his terms carefully in this matter, so we cannot know with certainty what he means. But several other aspects of his ecotheology suggest a less-than-robust orthodoxy at work.

Gore comments that the verdict is still out whether or not God created an "appropriate technology" when he brought forth the human race—given our dismal ecological record and the prospects for doom (apart from Gore's "global Marshall Plan," that is). This statement may be taken as a kind of poetic device to invigorate our interest in the subject and to induce guilt over our betrayal of the earth, but if it is taken literally it questions the very wisdom of God's act of creating humans in his image and likeness (Gen. 1:26). Furthermore, it also seems to imply that earth might be better off without these troublesome human pests. Gore is ambiguous on this point, but his treatment sounds distressingly similar to that of the "deep ecologists" who make the planet as a living entity the object of primary concern and therefore value humans only contingently in relation to Mother Earth. Yet, to his credit, Gore does spend several pages elsewhere rejecting the deep ecologist position that humans have become a blight on the biosphere that should be excised in short order.[9]

The prophet Isaiah clearly declares that God fashioned and made the earth not to be empty but to be inhabited (Isa. 45:18). Humans were not an experimental afterthought; neither is our worth determined by how well we serve the holistic health of the impersonal whole. We are the "appropriate technology" when we are under God's lordship; we become "inappropriate" (that is, sinful) as we rebel against divine authority and so become estranged from God, ourselves, creation, and other people.

But Gore's ecotheology lacks a coherent doctrine of sin and the fall of humanity. His primary object of veneration and concern seems to be the earth. We "sin" against the planet through ignorance and greed, both of which Gore deems to be largely correctable through massive governmental activism and partially correctable through individual initiative and responsibility. Gore applies recent concepts concerning addiction and dysfunctional families to civilization as a whole, drawing parallels with our denial of the ecological crisis and our resulting addictions to whatever distracts us from this reality.

Despite shedding some light on the nature of certain problems, Gore's analysis exhibits at least three weaknesses. First, it is based on psychological therapeutic models that, although they are now in vogue, may prove less than enduring. The dysfunctional heyday already seems to be fading, with critics questioning many of its key assumptions.

Second, even if theories of dysfunction and addiction vindicate themselves, it is quite a leap to move from small family situations to an entire civilization. Gore is fond of invoking the correspondence of the microcosmic to the macrocosmic (e.g., the percentage of salt in our blood is roughly that of the salt in the oceans), but his analogy between families and civilization in toto may stem more from a fertile imagination than a cogent comparison.

Third, by likening civilization's response to ecological problems to psychological dysfunction, Gore (probably unintentionally) tends to demoralize his audience. By this I mean that the use of an essentially medical model of dysfunction puts the problem in the realm of mental illness rather than morality. Sickness requires therapy; immorality requires repentance. The penchant of modernity to psychologize and medicalize sin often undercuts our ability to recognize it for what it is and to take the appropriate response. If there is ecological breakdown due to human mismanagement and greed (and there surely is, whether or not we endorse all of Gore's analysis), this situation demands moral repentance and reconciliation, not psychological speculation.

But the root of the ecological crisis, for Gore, seems more epistemological than ethical. He says that if only we could see the earth in its entirety we could better see the image of God. Here Gore extends the image of God from humankind in particular to creation in general. Twice he invokes the hologram, a popular New Age pedagogical device, for cosmological explication. In a hologram each part of a three-dimensional projected image cryptically contains the entire image. In other words, the whole is reflected and reproduced in miniature in the parts. New Age theorists such as George Leonard and Marilyn Ferguson have made much of this image and have argued or at least asserted that the whole universe might be a hologram. That is to say, all is one (monism).

Gore seems to want to retain some distinction between the Creator and the creation in that he says that the entire creation gives us an image of God, rather than saying the creation is God (pantheism). Nevertheless, his holographic theology both devalues humanity and falsely exalts the nonhuman creation. Biblically understood, all of creation is an expression of God's will and wisdom and as such reveals something of the Creator (Rom. 1:18–20; Ps. 19:1–6). Yet in the creation account of Genesis, humans alone are reckoned to be made in the image and likeness of God (Gen. 1:26). Though the entire nonhuman world is deemed "good" by the Creator, he declares his finished creation, now crowned by humanity, as "very good" (Gen. 1:31).

Although all of creation is to be valued and respected as God's handiwork, biblical cosmology reveals a hierarchy of dignity and value in which humans are at the apex of creation, yet always under the sovereignty of the Creator who charges them to tend the garden (cultivation and conservation) and to have dominion (development). Whatever the pedagogical uses of the hologram might be, theological revisionism ought not be one of them.

Gore also treads on dangerous ground when he expands his theology to find ecological principles in all the world's religions. We wonder what Gore's commitment to orthodoxy could be when he says, "The richness and diversity of our religious tradition throughout history is a spiritual resource long ignored by people of faith [read: Christians], who are often afraid to open their minds to teachings first offered outside their own system of belief" (p. 258). It is one thing to recognize some truth outside of one's religion if that truth agrees with the central tenets of one's religion. It is something else entirely to recognize truths that conflict with one's own tradition; in that case one has betrayed the faith.

Yet Gore's treatment attempts to honor all religious traditions as earth-honoring. Thus he approvingly cites American Indian religion, Hinduism, Buddhism, Islam, the Sufis, and the Baha'i faith as suitable theological resources for a sound ecotheology. But this strategy should be questioned on at least two grounds.

First, because of their often widely divergent metaphysics and cosmologies, not all religions do equally honor the earth. Significant strains of Hinduism such as the Advaita Vedanta school deem the space-time-material cosmos as ultimately illusory (*maya*) and so unworthy of reverent attention. The illusory world of maya must be transcended through yogic meditation to discover the true Self (or Brahman) within the soul. Much of Buddhism (the Theravadic school) is atheistic and so has no theology of creation; its cosmology claims that all existence is momentary, transient, and insubstantial. In essence, there is no essence to anything, only happenings or events. There is not nature as such, because nature implies a substantial and enduring existence over time and this is just what Theravada Buddhism denies.[10] Many other examples could be given, but the upshot is that building an ecumenical and ecological theology is far more difficult than Gore imagines. One can find teachings on the environment in every religion; finding substantial agreement on these teachings across traditions is another issue entirely.

Second, Gore should realize that because religions affirm different things about God, the earth, humanity, and salvation they cannot be integrated into one coherent world theology. I cannot view Hindu pantheism/polytheism as a "spiritual resource" (as Gore puts it) if I am an orthodox Christian. I must reject it. Neither can a devout Hindu accept the atheism of Theravada Buddhism. He must reject it.

Gore's attempt at ecological syncretism is especially strained and even incoherent when he approvingly cites recent studies by Marija Gimbutas and Raine Eisler that claim that the worship of the earth goddess predates monotheism. The speculation is that a peace-loving and ecologically balanced religion and culture of goddess worship was uprooted by a later monotheism stressing a masculine and domineering deity. The recent popularity of these speculations seems better explained by ideological animus than by the cogency of the historical evidence,[11] but if this goddess revisionism is correct, monotheism is necessary reduced to an illegitimate usurper of the goddesses.[12]

Even though he admits that the goddess religions probably contained "barbaric practices," Gore claims that "it seems obvious that a better understanding of a religious heritage preceding our own by so many thousands of years could offer us new insights into the nature of human existence" (p. 260). It seems more obvious that antiquity is no guarantee for wisdom, particularly when it comes to earth-worshiping idolaters (Rom. 1:18–32).

Gore cannot simultaneously appreciate a pantheistic goddess religion and also conserve the Christian view of a personal God who is transcendent over the creation. By accepting the primeval goddess theories, Gore cuts his own theological throat—that is, if he adheres to classical Christian theism.

Consensus-building may be a wise political strategy in Washington, D.C., but it is unwise in the realm of world religions—especially if one claims to follow a man who said "I am the way and the truth and the life. No one comes to the Father except through me" (John 14:6).

Gore and Prenatal Ecology

Gore's greatest failing in balancing his roles as politician, environmentalist, and Christian is a conspicuous sin of omission. His would-be tour de force says nothing about the ecological sanctity of the unborn and their place in the overall scheme of the environment. His only revelation on abortion is the following: "Personally, I favor the right of a woman to choose whether to conceive and have a child" (p. 316). He later says he opposes the coerced abortions in China and is troubled by countries where abortion rates are high because birth control is not available. Gore spends much time heralding the necessity of better birth control to take the strain off natural resources, but never discusses abortion as a problem worth addressing on its own terms.

Although the book is silent on this, Gore has formerly supported restrictions on abortions. While in the House of Representatives he consistently voted against federally funded abortions. In 1984 he also voted for an amendment to the Age Discrimination Act that would have defined "person" so as to include "unborn children from the moment of conception."[13]

But since moving to the Senate and aspiring to the presidency his views have changed and he has heralded the justice of the "Freedom of Choice Act," a legislative attempt to implement the most liberal reading of *Roe v. Wade.* This act, if signed by the president, would eliminate with a stroke of the pen virtually all legal restrictions now placed on abortion in all fifty states, such as informed consent, parental consent, waiting periods, or spousal consent. It would wipe out many if not all of the pro-life legal victories of the last twenty years since the tragedy of *Roe v. Wade.*

As a Christian, Gore should esteem the biblical revelation that teaches that all humans, born and unborn, are made in the image and likeness of God and so are worthy of respect. He should recognize that a just God calls for just laws that protect the innocent from violent extermination. Gore does not recognize these things, despite the fact that he waxes prophetic about the tragedy of wasted human lives in a chapter on material waste. He says: "If we have come to see the things we use as disposable, have we similarly transformed the way we think about our fellow human beings?" He then laments our devaluation of "latch key children, abandoned spouses, neglected friends and neighbors, [and] indeed any of our fellow citizens," especially "throw away children who are thrown out of their homes because they are too difficult to handle or because their parents no longer have the extra time for their special needs." Gore underscores all this by declaring his strong belief that "*the worst of all forms of pollution is wasted lives*" (pp. 161–62).

What could better illustrate "wasted lives" than the wholesale legal slaughter of one and half million unborn human beings every year in the United States? What could better illustrate a society's mentality than the disposal of unwanted human beings? It is ironic that Gore cites the biblical passage about Cain and Abel from Genesis 4—but not in relation to abortion. He says, "The first instance of 'pollution' in the Bible occurs when Cain slays Abel and his blood fall on the ground, rendering it fallow" (p. 247). The Scriptures declare that the blood of Abel cries out from the ground for divine judgment. Whatever judgment humans deserve for nonhuman ecological devastation pales in comparison to the deafening roar of the river of aborted blood calling out to a just God for justice. Gore is deaf to this roar; he is more concerned about preserving an ecological niche for the spotted owl than he is about the precarious prenatal niche of the unborn in America and throughout the planet. It is exceedingly odd that one who so adamantly argues for a greater sense of "connectedness to nature" would champion a public policy that allows the unrestricted severing of the connection between mother and child through abortion. This brutal fact alone disqualifies Gore from being an ecologist whose thinking is consistent with the deepest insights of Christian ethics. Prenatal ecology is not his concern.

One who aspires to fulfill the trinitarian role of politician, environmentalist, and Christian aspires to a challenging and demanding endeavor. M. Scott Peck, who endorses the book on the back cover, seems to believe that Gore gloriously succeeds in this task. Not fearing hyperbole, he comments that *Earth in the Balance* is "a brilliantly written, prophetic, even a holy book." Yet despite the passion, dedication, and encyclopedic ambitions Gore displayed in *Earth in the Balance,* we must look elsewhere for a "prophetic and even a holy book" that wisely balances the concerns of a politician, an environmentalist, and a Christian.

Part **Four**

Evangelism

24

Gurdjieff

G. I. Gurdjieff (1877–1949) was seen by many, according to his follower J. G. Bennett, as "a very great enigma." His charisma and eclectic philosophy continue to entice and enamour many a "seeker of truth." He has a special appeal to elitist intellectuals. Although this Russian mystic sought and taught esotericism ("knowledge for the few"), sociologist Robert Ellwood commented that Gurdjieff "probably influenced Western cults and esotericism more than any other modern figure except Madame Blavatsky [founder of Theosophy]."

Gurdjieff's influence continues through his and his followers' writings and several "Gurdjieff-Ouspensky Schools" across the country. Those affected by Gurdjieff's ideas include novelists Katherine Mansfield and Rudyard Kipling, architect Frank Lloyd Wright and, more recently, philosopher Jacob Needleman and jazz musician Keith Jarrett.

His teaching along with the romanticized legend of his "quest for truth" (in 1979 made into the movie *Meetings with Remarkable Men*) present a tantalizing option for those disenchanted with the common and the popular—those who are themselves in search of "remarkable men," whether purported avatars, swamis, or gurus. Part of Gurdjieff's magnetism consisted in the totality and universality of his claims. In the preface to his *All and Everything: Beelzebub's Tales to His Grandson,* he states that his purpose is to "destroy mercilessly the beliefs and views rooted for centuries in the mind and feeling of man." How was this to be done? How could one find "the esoteric truth?"

Gurdjieff and his short-time cohort P. D. Ouspensky (Russian philosopher and theoretical mathematician) found a radical problem in humanity: we are "asleep," naturally spiritually dead, mere machines, imprisoned by merely automatic behavior. Self-knowledge and self-development (called by Gurdjieff "work on oneself") could, with proper instruction and ardor, release inner possibilities and the chance for immorality. One climbs the seven-step ladder of consciousness to truth by self-effort, from "basic waking states" on through other steps and finally to "Complete Man" where the individual is "immortal with the limits of the solar system."

Gurdjieff saw this as no easy task, as was illustrated by a sign above his door at his Institute for the Harmonious Development of Man (1922–1933) in Fontaineblue, France: "It is useless to pass through these doors unless you have well-developed critical faculties." The gospel of Gurdjieff is one of intense and bizarre self-effort, including specialized dances, meditation, and strange diets.

No humble soul, Gurdjieff was also famous for his raucous living and intimidating, if not mesmerizing, presence.

The combination of Gnostic, Sufi, Buddhist, and occultic philosophies Gurdjieff called "esoteric Christianity"—which he clearly distinguished from biblical Christianity. Christ, Gurdjieff claimed, was a magician, someone having esoteric-occultic knowledge but who was not uniquely the God-man.

Meet Another Remarkable Man

Any "seeker of truth" should be interested in the remarkable person of Jesus Christ, whose claims, like Gurdjieff's, are total and universal.

Christ also saw a radical problem at the core of humanity; he too saw people as spiritually dead and in desperate need of spiritual life. He saw the problem as a natural selfishness and pride of heart that alienated people from a morally perfect God: "Out of the heart come evil thoughts, sexual immorality, theft, murder, adultery, greed, malice, deceit, lewdness, envy, slander, arrogance and folly" (Mark 7:21–22). This is the problem of sin. Humanity is not naturally right with God. God is displeased with our rebellion against him, because we do not, as Jesus commanded, love him with our whole being.

Jesus' answer to our radical problem was not laborious self-development. The dead don't grow; they only decay. A radical cure is needed for a radical problem, a cure from outside the self—from God himself. And, amazingly, the cure is without price! It is a gift to be received by faith in Christ himself. Jesus claimed the authority to forgive sin and give spiritual life. He says, "For God so loved the world that he gave his one and only Son, that whoever believes in him shall not perish but have eternal life" (John 3:16). There is good news for the spiritually dead. They can be born again of the Spirit of God (John 3).

Jesus' agonizing death on the cross and his resurrection from the dead proclaim that he not only bore the penalty for the sin of the world, but also triumphed over sin, death, and the grave. Christ's disciples have peace with God and hope for this life and the next.

Jesus anchored his claims with authority. He said, "I am the way and the truth and the life. No one comes to the Father except by me" (John 14:6). And also, "I am the light of the world. Whoever follows me will never walk in darkness, but will have the light of life" (John 8:12). Instead of teaching "esoteric truth," a secret doctrine only for the few, he said, "I have spoken openly to the world" (John 18:20). His teaching was public and his disciples gathered publicly; in fact, he sent his disciples to bring his message to all the world (Matt. 28:18–20). He spoke not as an occultist, but as God made flesh, God personally entering the stage of history for his erring children's redemption.

Gurdjieff called his seekers to discipleship. So does Jesus Christ. But instead of saying, as did Gurdjieff, "It is useless . . . unless you have well-developed critical faculties," Christ says, "Come to me, all you who are weary and burdened, and I will give you rest. Take my yoke upon you and learn from me, for I am gentle and humble in heart, and you will find rest for your souls. For my yoke is easy and my burden is light" (Matt. 11:28–30).

25

New Age Christmas

A few Christmases ago I happily brought home a new compact disk with a variety of instrumental Christmas songs. But my wife objected that something about the music was not quite right. Upon reading the liner notes we found that several of the musicians had decidedly New Age views of Christmas. David Lanz wrote that the essence of Christmas is "the rebirth of the Christ within."

For New Age musician Lanz, Christmas means the discovery of the Christ within us all. Never mind "away in a manger"; the real Christmas story is autobiographical. According to New Age teachings, Jesus was not born as "Christ the Lord," as the Gospels announce, but as a baby who would later attain to Christ consciousness. He is not the unique Messiah, Immanuel (God with us), but one of many enlightened beings who serve as examples for our own evolution. A New Age Christmas celebrates "the rebirth of the Christ within," not the birth of the Christ of history.

Instead of commemorating the advent of "God with us" we attempt to recover the God who is us. The birth of Jesus is merely an occasion to reflect on our own potential as gods and goddesses

183

in the making. As Joseph Campbell put it, we are all incarnations of God—only some of us have not yet realized it.

What is at stake is a clash of world views. Historic Christianity teaches that God is a personal being who created the universe distinct from himself. Out of love, God sent Jesus, his one and only son, into the world to provide redemption for those who would accept his death on the cross as the atonement for their sins and believe in his resurrection as their source of eternal life.

New Age theology exchanges the personal God of Christianity for an impersonal Force, Principle, or Consciousness. Humans can tap into this Force through a change in consciousness and realize their own divinity, as did Jesus and other mystical masters. But there is no need for the forgiveness of sin because there is no sin to forgive and no personal, loving God to provide a sacrifice for it. An impersonal God cannot love anyone.

Before the New Age steals your Christmas, consider these points. The New Testament documents, all written by eyewitnesses of the events described or by those who had access to eyewitnesses, leave no room for the New Age interpretation of Jesus. For these authorities, Jesus is God with us, the Messiah. He alone is "Lord at his birth." Read it for yourself.

Instead of looking for "the Christ within," consider the credentials of the New Testament Christ. He healed the sick, raised the dead, forgave sin, preached with power, loved the lowly, was worshiped at his birth and during his ministry, and was raised from the dead. Is this one of many mystical masters? Are we on his level? Or is Jesus Christ the one Mediator between God and humanity, as the apostle Paul taught (1 Tim. 2:5)?

As G. K. Chesterton said, belief in the God within easily degenerates into the worship of oneself. The search for a divine self may seem a romantic and noble quest, but according to Jesus it is the epitome of futility. Jesus Christ redirects our attention when he says: "I am the way and the truth and the life. No one comes to the Father except through me" (John 14:6). The self is a poor substitute for the Savior.

Christmas in the New Age is a season without the supreme gift God gave to humanity: Jesus Christ himself. This is one gift that should not be exchanged.

26

Reincarnation or Resurrection?

Throughout human history people have wondered what if anything lies beyond the grave. Is death the end of existence, an entry into eternity, or an intermission between earthly lives? These questions have intrigued and haunted mortals for the millennia.

Eastern religions teach that the soul reincarnates in many different bodies. Because of the influence of the New Age movement, approximately 25 percent of Americans now believe in reincarnation. Celebrities such as actress Shirley MacLaine and country singer Willie Nelson believe they have lived before and will live again. Why are so many people drawn to reincarnation?

The Appeal of Reincarnation

Reincarnation offers hope to many. If we don't "get it right" in this life, we have another chance the next time around. Some even consult therapists in the hope of learning details of their past lives that may help them solve their present problems.

Reincarnation also claims to insure justice in human affairs. We get what we deserve in every life. In Eastern religions, reincarnation is connected with the law of karma; it teaches that good deeds from past lives produce rewards in the next life or lives. Bad deeds produce punishments in the next life or lives. The law of karma is understood as an unbending and impersonal rule of the universe. We all get what we deserve. This consoles some who agonize over the apparent injustices in the world. And by working off one's bad karma over many lifetimes, a person can finally escape the process of rebirth and attain enlightenment.

Can reincarnation realistically offer hope and a sense of justice to a troubled world? Can it answer the nagging problem of death and what lies beyond?

Questioning Reincarnation

We should take a second look at reincarnation. Even reincarnationists admit that the vast majority of humans do not remember their previous lives. Yet how can we learn from our past mistakes if we cannot remember them? We seem to make the same mistakes over and over again. The second chances don't appear to be doing us much good. Given the moral failure rate of human history, do we have any reason to hope that we will get it right in a future lifetime? Where is the basis for such optimism?

In cultures such as India, the law of karma has justified not helping those suffering because it is thought that they are working off their bad karma. The lowest social class in India, the Untouchables, have been traditionally viewed as deserving their fate because of actions in previous lives. To help an Untouchable would be like releasing a guilty prisoner who had served but a small portion of his jail term.

According to reincarnation, the innocent do not suffer. All suffering is deserved on the basis of bad karma. The baby born without legs deserved it, as did the woman who was raped. There is no injustice and no forgiveness. None are innocent, and there is no grace available—only the demands of karma.

Such teaching undercuts the basis for compassion in this life and makes the prospect for future lives less than heavenly for those without a perfect track record. Every wrongdoing will be punished without forgiveness, and no one can help you along the way. This is not good news.

Karma or Gospel?

The law of karma is unmerciful, yet the message of Jesus Christ is entirely different. Jesus taught that no one can keep the moral law. The human heart is unclean because of wrong attitudes and actions. Yet he never spoke of the law of karma as a cosmic mechanism assigning rewards and punishments. For Jesus, wrongdoing is an offense against a loving and absolutely good God, who created the universe and each person in it.

Jesus never encouraged anyone to try to build up good karma from lifetime to lifetime in order to find enlightenment. Jesus said, "I tell you the truth, everyone who sins is a slave to sin" (John 8:34). Given the depth of human sin, saving oneself through good karma would be like trying to build a ladder out of water.

Jesus spoke of people receiving either eternal reward or eternal punishment according to how they responded to him during their *one* lifetime on earth (Matt. 25:31–46; see also Heb. 9:27). He also declared that he would raise the dead at the end of history; those who believed in him would experience life, those who rejected him would be condemned (John 5:24–29). This teaching leaves no room for reincarnation.

But how can someone enslaved to sin find hope if not in reincarnation? How can eternal life be received?

Jesus proclaimed that he came into the world "to seek and to save what was lost" (Luke 19:10). Through his ministry of teaching, preaching, and healing, he demonstrated a sinless life and the power over death itself by raising the dead. He said about himself, "The Son of Man did not come to be served, but to serve, and to give his life as a ransom for many" (Mark 10:45). He came to touch the untouchables as no one else could. He can do the same today.

Jesus gave his life for humanity by going to the cross to die. The apostle Paul said this about Jesus: "God made him who had no sin to be sin for us, so that in him we might become the righteousness of God" (2 Cor. 5:21). Jesus also instructed his disciples that his body and blood would be given for the forgiveness of sin (Luke 22:19–20).

Jesus showed his forgiving love even on the bloodstained cross. A criminal on a cross next to Jesus confessed his sin and asked Jesus to remember him. Jesus responded, "I tell you the truth, today you will be with me in paradise" (Luke 23:43). Only faith in Jesus was required for paradise, not lifetime after lifetime of working off bad karma and building up good karma.

Good News or Bad News?

The message of reincarnation is ultimately bad news. You must earn your own salvation through countless lifetimes and no one can help you. The message of Jesus is good news. No, you can't save yourself. But Jesus left heaven and came to earth to rescue you. He died to pay the just penalty for your sin. He rose from the dead to demonstrate his authority as the Son of God (Rom. 1:4). And he asks you to turn from your old ways to follow him. He said: "For God so loved the world that he gave his one and only Son, that whoever believes in him shall not perish but have eternal life" (John 3:16).

All who believe in him and give their lives to him are freed from the fear of death and the penalty of sin. They can rejoice in these words of Jesus: "I am the resurrection and the life. He who believes in me will live, even though he dies; and whoever lives and believes in me will never die" (John 11:25–26).

27

New Age, New Life

I am God! I am God!" shouted actress Shirley MacLaine in her autobiographical miniseries, *Out on a Limb*. The 1987 television series was based on her best-selling book of the same name and thrust the New Age movement into the national spotlight. Her striking declaration has been buzzing in the minds of scores of people captivated by her romantic story of spiritual enlightenment. Two more best-selling spiritual autobiographies followed—*Dancing in the Light* and *It's All in the Playing*—which celebrated the enchantments of the New Age experience, whether it be spirit contact, reincarnation, or out-of-the-body experiences. Her newer book, *Going Within*, gives instruction on cultivating inner strength through yoga and meditation.

MacLaine is not a lone voice crying in the wilderness, but one of a growing chorus of New Age converts reviving an "ancient wisdom" for the modern masses. Their promise is alluring and their claim astounding: We are no mere mortals. We can create our own reality as gods and goddesses. In the popular television series and book *The Power of Myth* (1988), professor Joseph Campbell proclaimed that "each of us is the incarnation of God," not Jesus only. "We are all manifestations of the Buddha consciousness or Christ consciousness, only we don't know it," he asserted.

But is this in agreement with Christianity? Some think so. While in a Christian book store, I met a woman who called herself a "New Age Christian" who told me that Jesus taught reincarnation because he said that John the Baptist was really the Old Testament prophet Elijah. I mentioned that Jesus wasn't speaking literally because Elijah, according to the Old Testament (2 Kings 2) never died but was taken directly to heaven. He never gave over his soul to be recycled (reincarnated) as John the Baptist. Besides that, I added, John the Baptist himself denied being the literal Elijah (John 1:21) and Jesus never taught reincarnation but affirmed that the dead would be resurrected once and for all in physical bodies that would spend eternity in heaven or hell. My "New Age Christian" friend pondered this a bit before leaving the store.

More Than Mere Mortals?

But what is "the New Age movement" promoted by MacLaine, Campbell, and "New Age Christians"? It is an umbrella term covering a wide variety of events, ideas, people, practices, and organizations. Those involved speak much of "networking" with each other for the purposes of personal and social transformation. The "movement" is better viewed as a shift in the public mindset than as a comprehensive and tightly run conspiracy. Nevertheless, its influence is felt everywhere from business seminars to public education to medical care to the movies. The essence of the New Age mindset can be distilled into a few core ideas that we will review before testing its expansive promises.

First, the New Age movement has an upbeat and optimistic spirit: a New Age of peace, love, and tranquility is dawning. In astrology this is referred to as "the Age of Aquarius." Our planet's present economic, ecological, political, and military crises can and must be overcome through a "change in consciousness" that involves a new mindset and a new mystical experience. Some captured by the New Age vision look for a great world leader (sometimes called "the Christ") to bring peace; but they do not mean the Jesus of the Bible, as we will see.

Second, the New Age proclaims "the God within" us all. "I am God!" cries MacLaine, as do countless others. Drawing from the teachings of Eastern mysticism and occultism, the New Age mindset sees everything as divine. All that is, is God. All is one with God. God is not a personal and moral Being, but rather an impersonal principle, vibration, or essence like "the Force" of *Star Wars* and its sequels. The New Age challenges us to awaken our "God consciousness" through various mystical methods such as Transcendental Meditation, Silva Mind Control, yoga, self-hypnosis, visualization, or participation in consciousness-raising programs such as Lifespring or the Forum. We all have divine potential but few have tapped into it successfully. So we find hundreds of New Age self-help books and programs to summon the sleeping savior within.

Third, the New Age heralds that humans have unlimited potential. Everything is possible with us! Only ignorance of our divinity drags us down. As divine beings, the paranormal beckons us: esp, telepathy, contact with "spirit guides" (channeling), and out-of-the-body experiences become desirable. We are miracles waiting to happen. MacLaine teaches that "we are unlimited, we just don't know it." (We are gods who somehow forgot that we are gods . . .) And if we don't "master the possibilities" of godhood in this life, reincarnation assures us that we will have endless other opportunities for advancement. The idea of a final judgment before a holy and just God is deemed old-fashioned and too . . . well, judgmental. So is the idea of sin, which is viewed an outmoded notion causing guilt feelings unbecoming of divine beings.

Fourth, there is a strong tendency in New Age circles to deny objective and absolute standards of morality. I once spoke with a man who assured me that because everyone's soul is divine, we can do no evil. I asked him if this was true of Hitler, and he answered, "Yes, Hitler wasn't really evil, because he was divine in essence and because good and evil are one in God. Even Lucifer is a part of God." Campbell taught that God is beyond any notion of good and evil and that we must accept everything that happens without judgment. A prominent New Age writer, W. Brugh Joy, teaches that "absolutes are a concoction of the rational mind." This stems from the New Age belief that God is not a just and good Creator, but merely an impersonal force without moral attributes. *It* just is.

The New Age vision of a world restored through tapping into the energy of the unlimited is enticing and intriguing. Are we more than mere mortals?

Spiritual Differences

New Age "open-mindedness" notwithstanding, biblical teaching stands at odds with the New Age mindset. Not everything billed as spiritual is of the same spirit. The differences are real and important.

From the first to the last book of the Bible, the supreme Spirit is shown to be the personal and living Lord of the universe. When God revealed himself to Moses in the burning bush, he declared, "I AM WHO I AM" (Exod. 3:14). God speaks as a personal being, a center of consciousness. The Bible never presents God as an impersonal abstraction such as a principle, essence, or force. God is not an It, but a Person.

God performs the acts of a personal being. A reading of the Bible will show that God creates, God hears, God speaks, God judges, God forgives. He is. He is not to be identified with his creation. The apostle Paul highlights this when he wrote of those who deny God: "They exchanged the truth of God for a lie, and worshiped and served created things rather than the Creator—who is forever praised" (Rom. 1:25). For Paul, all is not God; but all should praise the Creator, who alone is God.

As creatures, we do not possess the credentials of the Creator. Humans are more like God than anything else in the universe. We are "wonderfully made" (Ps. 139) in his image and likeness (Gen. 1:26). Yet we fall infinitely short of godhood. God spoke through the prophet Ezekiel to the king of Tyre, an ancient God-imposter:

In the pride of your heart you say, "I am a god; I sit on the throne of a god in the heart of the seas." But you are a man and not a god, though you think you are as wise as a god. [Ezek. 28:2]

God pronounces his judgment on such foolish pride and asks this stubborn God-player: "Will you then say, 'I am a god,' in the presence of those who kill you? You will be but a man, not a god, in the hands of those who slay you" (v. 9). When MacLaine exclaims, "I am God," the great I Am knows better. As he declared through his prophet Isaiah: "I am God, and there is no other; I am God, and there is none like me" (Isa. 46:9).

Consider some basic facts: God is everywhere simultaneously (without being everything); but we can only be one place at any given time (if that!). God is all-powerful; we are limited by our creaturehood. God knows everything; we know only in part. God is morally perfect; we are all quite clearly less than true to our own consciences. We certainly deserve a failing grade in divinity.

If God is holy and just, then our moral failings put us out of step with his character and purposes. Jesus never taught that humans suffered from a lack of knowledge of their true nature as divine. Rather, he accurately diagnosed the problem as one of ethical wrongdoing. He located the root of moral uncleanness squarely in the human heart. He said:

For from within, out of men's hearts, come evil thoughts, sexual immorality, theft, murder, adultery, greed, malice, deceit, lewdness, envy, slander, arrogance and folly. All these evils come from inside and make a man "unclean." [Mark 7:21–22]

Jesus also knew that this uncleanness was not an occasional problem but a general condition of humanity. He said, "I tell you the truth, everyone who sins is a slave to sin" (John 8:34). Those who are prone to view sin as only severe wrongdoings such as murder and theft should consider Jesus' standards. His rule of moral goodness was: "'love the Lord your God with all your heart and with all your soul and with all your mind'" and "'love your neighbor as yourself'" (Matt. 22:37, 39). Who can live up to God's perfect standard of goodness?

Jesus: Guru or Lord?

Those in the New Age movement highly esteem Jesus as a great teacher, master, guru, or yogi. Yet the Jesus of the New Testament does not echo the message of the New Age. He did not claim to be an example of a self-realized guru, but the unique and un-repeatable revelation of a personal God. He said about himself, "The Son of Man came to seek and to save what was lost" (Luke 19:10). Jesus was on a rescue mission to planet Earth to save those lost in sin, those who cannot live up to God's requirements. Jesus also proclaimed that "the Son of Man did not come to be served, but to serve, and to give his life as a ransom for many" (Mark 10:45).

While those involved in the New Age claim to tap into their deity (with varying degrees of success), Jesus demonstrated his deity in ways never approached by any other historical figure. He performed countless miracles over nature, over sickness, and over death itself when he raised his friend Lazarus from the dead. The deaf heard, the blind saw, the crippled leaped for joy. He taught with an undeniable authority that either commanded respect or fueled hatred from those who could not bear pure truth. He claimed to be no less than God in human form when he said he had the authority on earth to forgive sins (Mark 2:1–12). When he declared, "Before Abraham was born, I am" (John 8:58) he used the divine title *I Am* for himself and his audi-ence knew it.

Jesus was so bold as to divide all people in terms of their response to him. He said, "He who is not with me is against me, and he who does not gather with me scatters" (Matt. 12:30). Jesus invited his hearers to place their faith in him and to commit themselves to him alone. He said, "For God so loved the world that he gave his one and only Son, that whoever believes in him shall not perish but have eternal life" (John 3:16).

When his disciples asked him the way to God, the Father, Jesus uttered as clear a statement about his identity and mission as can be imagined. He said, "I am the way and the truth and the life. No one comes to the Father except through me" (John 14:6). Only Jesus had the credentials to make this claim stick. He laid down his life for those needing new life. "I am the good shepherd," he said. "The good shepherd lays down his life for the sheep" (John 10:11).

This is the meaning of Jesus' crucifixion. Although he had the authority to call down legions of angels to deliver him from death, he chose to offer his life as a sacrifice for the sheep who had strayed. As the apostle Paul put it, though Jesus Christ was rich in heaven before his incarnation, he left heaven for earth and became poor in order to make us rich (2 Cor. 8:9). Paul further explains the deep love of God shown in Jesus Christ:

> You see, at just the right time, when we were still powerless, Christ died for the ungodly. Very rarely will anyone die for a righteous man, though for a good man someone might possibly dare to die. But God demonstrates his own love for us in this: While we were still sinners, Christ died for us. [Rom. 5:6–8]

Jesus' death on the cross was given as "a ransom for many." In his death, he who was sinless and perfect paid the penalty for human sin. Paul makes this clear: "God made him who had no sin to be sin for us, so that in him we might become the righteousness of God" (2 Cor. 5:21).

Although those in the New Age think of the idea of sin as negative and limiting, we must take it seriously if we are to understand Jesus Christ. The life, teachings, and death of Jesus dissolve into nonsense without the true meaning of sin. Jesus came to die for our sins in order to set us right with God. Here is the great divide between New Age spirituality and the message of Jesus.

The God of the New Age is an impersonal and amorphous abstraction that loves nothing and feels nothing. An Energy Source can't ever show compassion. It can't die in order to save us. Being impersonal, it can't even relate to us person to person. But Jesus declared that he came into the world in love to rescue those enslaved to sin. God, the personal Lord, cared enough to make a provision for our sorry state. And a just God required no less than a perfect sacrifice for the forgiveness of sin. Jesus offered his life for ours and in doing so defeated the power of sin and

Satan himself. As the apostle John said, "The Son of God came to destroy the works of the devil" (1 John 3:8). That is God's love in action.

To vindicate his claims, Jesus did what no one else has ever done. After three days in a tomb, he rose from the dead never to die again, just as he predicted. Even before his death, Jesus was certain of his victory over death, sin, and the devil. He proclaimed: "I am the resurrection and the life. He who believes in me will live, even though he dies; and whoever lives and believes in me will never die" (John 11:25).

Jesus offered no hope in reincarnation as a way to find liberation. He pointed people to himself for life eternal. To find him was to find life, to reject him to lose life. He says: "Whoever acknowledges me before men, I will also acknowledge him before my Father in heaven. But whoever disowns me before men, I will disown him before my Father in heaven" (Matt. 10:32–33).

In Jesus and in Jesus alone can we find hope for new life, hope, and peace. His followers know the joy of being forgiven of their sins and welcomed into fellowship with God himself. In light of the supremacy of Jesus Christ, the trappings of the New Age fall into insignificance. They are, in fact, dangerous diversions from spiritual reality. Jesus himself refers to those who do persist in practicing "magic arts" (the occult) as being lost in hell (Rev. 22:15). While the New Age promises godhood and unlimited potential through self-discovery and occult experimentation, Jesus promises himself as the final satisfaction: "If anyone is thirsty, let him come to me and drink. Whoever believes in me, as the Scripture said, streams of living water will flow from within him" (John 7:37–38).

Instead of looking within for unlimited power, we can look to Jesus for strength, wisdom, and direction. The apostle Paul knew this well when he said that "we have this treasure in jars of clay to show that this all-surpassing power is from God and not from us" (2 Cor. 4:7). Those who know this power from God are impressed to make Jesus known and to live out his principles in service to a needy world.

The Way to Life

But this life-giving, resurrected Jesus asks something from us—namely, everything. Mere mortals find their value and significance only by serving their Sovereign, not by pretending to be sovereign. This is what we were meant to do. So Jesus says, "Whoever finds his life will lose it, and whoever loses his life for my sake will find it" (Matt. 10:39). If we live for ourselves we ultimately lose all. If we live for the one who created us and gives us life eternal, we gain all.

The apostle Peter proclaimed of Jesus, "Salvation is found in no one else, for there is no other name under heaven given to men by which we must be saved" (Acts 4:12). This salvation cannot be earned, nor is it found within. It can be received only as a loving gift by having faith in what Jesus has done through his death and resurrection.

If you want to submit to the guidance and authority of this loving Jesus, be assured that he will hear and answer your prayer.

> Lord Jesus, I cannot save myself. I have not looked to you for strength and hope and life. I have sinned and fallen short of your perfect standards. I renounce all New Age practices which are displeasing to you. I am not God. I turn away from my futile quest for godhood. Please forgive me. I believe that you died for my sin and that you were raised from the dead. I confess you as the Lord of the universe and of my life. I trust you to forgive my sins and teach me how to live for you. Thank you for hearing my prayer. Amen.

Books for a Christian Mind
An Annotated Bibliography

For the bibliophile, of the making of bibliographies there is no end. This bibliography makes no claim to be exhaustive concerning either the topics addressed or the books within those categories. I have selected books that I take to be pivotal in developing a Christian mind with respect to the issues mentioned in this book. Most of these books are written from a Christian perspective, but even those that are not should still help contribute to a Christian world view. At the end I have also added a partial listing of Christian organizations that seek to apply a Christian world view to our culture.

Christian Doctrine

Athanasius. *The Incarnation of the Word.* New York: Macmillan, 1946. A classic on Christology from the fourth century. Features an insightful introduction by C. S. Lewis.

Bowman, Robert M. *Orthodoxy and Heresy: A Biblical Guide to Doctrinal Discernment.* Grand Rapids: Baker, 1992. Explains the importance of biblical doctrine and how to discern doctrinal error in a variety of forms. Not so much a summary of doctrine as a call to discernment.

Brown, Harold O. J. *Heresies: The Image of Christ in the Mirror of Heresy and Orthodoxy from the Apostles to the Present.* Garden City, N.Y.: Doubleday, 1984. A comprehensive study of heresy and orthodoxy throughout history.

Calvin, John. *Institutes of the Christian Religion.* Many different editions. The more recent the edition, the more readable the translation will probably be. Calvin is often criticized unfairly and his ideas caricatured. But it must be remembered that he was the preeminent systematic theologian of the Reformation with a tremendous grasp of Scripture and a great talent for expositing it. The material on justification by faith is vital.

Elwell, Walter A., ed. *Topical Analysis of the Bible.* Grand Rapids: Baker, 1991. An excellent compendium of biblical texts organized around key doctrinal themes. A helpful tool.

Erickson, Millard J. *Christian Theology.* Grand Rapids: Baker, 1983–85. A clearly
    written and thorough treatment of Christian doctrine filled with helpful illus-
    trations and sound thinking. A major evangelical work in our day.
    ———. *Does It Matter What I Believe? What the Bible Teaches and Why We Should
    Believe It.* Grand Rapids: Baker, 1992. A fine introduction to doctrine writ-
    ten by a noteworthy theologian concerned to instruct the average church-
    goer.
    ———. *The Word Became Flesh: An Incarnational Christology.* Grand Rapids:
    Baker, 1991. A major work on Christology. Comprehensive and well written.
Grenz, Stanley. *The Millennial Maze: Sorting Out Evangelical Options.* Down-
    ers Grove: InterVarsity, 1992. A very well-documented and fairly presented
    survey on eschatology.
Lewis, Gordon, and Bruce Demarest. *Integrative Theology: Historical, Biblical,
    Systematic, Apologetic.* 3 vols. Grand Rapids: Zondervan, 1987–1994. Uses a
    unique and helpful fourfold format to systematically present Christian doc-
    trine in its historical, biblical, systematic, apologetic, and practical dimen-
    sions.
Little, Paul E. *Know What You Believe.* Wheaton: Victor, 1980. Good introduc-
    tory work.
MacArthur, John F. *The Gospel According to Jesus: What Does Jesus Mean When
    He Says "Follow Me"?* Grand Rapids: Zondervan, Academie Books, 1988.
    Cogently argues that true faith in Jesus will result in a changed life and good
    works.
Martin, Walter. *Essential Christianity: A Handbook on Basic Christian Doctrines.*
    Ventura, Calif.: Regal, 1980. Good introductory material by a cult expert.
Packer, J. I. *Knowing God.* Downers Grove: InterVarsity, 1993. Clear and deep
    teaching on the nature of God.
Rushdoony, R. J. *Foundations of Social Order: Studies in Creeds and Councils of
    the Early Church.* Fairfax, Va.: Thoburn, 1978. A study of the relationship
    between creedal theology and social order.
Sproul, R. C. *The Holiness of God.* Wheaton: Tyndale House, 1985. An impor-
    tant study on an undervalued doctrine.
Stott, John R. W. *Basic Christianity.* Downers Grove: InterVarsity, 1976. A clas-
    sic treatment. Good to give to interested non-Christians.
    ———. *The Cross of Christ.* Downers Grove: InterVarsity, 1986. A theological
    rich and devotionally challenging presentation of the doctrine of salvation.
Tozer, A. W. *The Knowledge of the Holy: The Attributes of God, Their Meaning in
    the Christian Life.* New York: Harper, 1961. A devotional and doctrinal clas-
    sic.

Apologetics and the Christian World View

Allen, Diogenes. *Three Outsiders: Soren Kierkegaard, Blaise Pascal, Simone Weil.*
    Cambridge, Mass.: Cowley Publications, 1983. A sympathetic treatment of
    three influential Christian thinkers.

Blamires, Harry. *The Christian Mind: How Should a Christian Think?* Ann Arbor: Servant, 1978. A classic treatment of how a Christian ought to think "Christianly."

Blomberg, Craig. *The Historical Reliability of the Gospels.* Downers Grove: InterVarsity, 1987. An excellent treatment of the trustworthiness of the gospels in light of modern scholarship.

Bruce, F. F. *The Canon of Scripture.* Downers Grove: InterVarsity, 1988. A clear and scholarly explanation of how we got our Bible by a seasoned scholar.

Carnell, E. J. *An Introduction to Christian Apologetics: A Philosophical Defense of the Trinitarian-Theistic Faith.* Grand Rapids: Eerdmans, 1948. An influential treatise written by a leader of the early evangelical movement.

Carson, D. A. *How Long, O Lord?: Reflections on Suffering and Evil.* Grand Rapids: Baker, 1990. A first-rate New Testament scholar wisely reflects on the problem of pain in human life and offers biblical answers.

Chesterton, G. K. *The Everlasting Man.* Garden City, N.Y.: Image Books, 1955. Christian apologetics as only Chesterton can deliver.

———. *Orthodoxy.* Garden City, N.Y.: Image Books, 1959. A witty and trenchant critique of modernity and defense of Christianity from 1908.

Clark, Gordon H. *A Christian View of Men and Things: An Introduction to Philosophy.* Grand Rapids: Baker, 1981. An introduction to philosophy from a Christian perspective by a noteworthy Christian philosopher.

Clark, Gordon H. *From Thales to Dewey: A History of Philosophy.* Jefferson, Md.: The Trinity Foundation, 1988. An excellent one volume history of philosophy from a Christian perspective.

Craig, William Lane. *Apologetics: An Introduction.* Chicago: Moody, 1984. A fine and well-documented introduction.

———. *Knowing the Truth about the Resurrection: Our Response to the Empty Tomb.* Ann Arbor: Servant, 1988. Probably the best nontechnical defense of the resurrection of Jesus available.

Cunningham, Richard B. *The Christian Faith and Its Contemporary Rivals.* Nashville: Broadman, 1988. A philosophically astute look at challenges to Christian faith, particularly naturalism.

Dooyeweerd, Herman. *Roots of Western Culture: Pagan, Secular, and Christian Options.* Toronto: Wedge, 1979. Probably the most approachable work by the polymathic Dutch philosopher. A Christian analysis of Western philosophical thought.

Dyrness, William. *Christian Apologetics in a World Community.* Downers Grove: InterVarsity, 1983. A good introductory work with an international focus.

Evans, C. Stephen. *Philosophy of Religion: Thinking about Faith.* Downers Grove: InterVarsity, 1985. An excellent introduction to the subject from a Christian viewpoint.

———. *The Quest for Faith: Reason and Mystery as Pointers to God.* Downers Grove: InterVarsity, 1986. A short but penetrating recommendation of Christianity.

Frame, John M. *The Doctrine of the Knowledge of God.* Phillipsburg, N.J.: Presbyterian and Reformed, 1987. A combination of apologetics and systematic theology by one of Van Til's more noteworthy students.

Geisler, Norman L. *Christian Apologetics.* Grand Rapids: Baker, 1981. A wide-ranging survey of various world views and apologetic methods.

———. *Miracles and the Modern Mind: A Defense of Biblical Miracles.* Grand Rapids: Baker, 1992. A clear and convincing defense of supernaturalism.

Habermas, Gary. *The Verdict of History.* Nashville: Nelson, 1988. Excellent material on Jesus and early Christianity culled from non-Christian sources.

Henry, Carl F. H. *God, Revelation, and Authority.* 6 vols. Waco: Word, 1976–1982. A major series on philosophical theology, apologetics, and biblical inerrancy. Vast in its range, deep in its erudition.

Holmes, Arthur F. *All Truth Is God's Truth.* Downers Grove: InterVarsity, 1983. A philosophical assessment of the Christian view of truth and knowing.

———. *Contours of a World View.* Grand Rapids: Eerdmans, 1983. A rich treatment of the Christian world view in relation to naturalism. The only drawback is a weak view of abortion.

Johnson, Paul. *Intellectuals.* New York: Harper and Row, 1988. Biographical studies of leading modern non-Christian intellectuals such as Rousseau, Marx, and Sartre that reveal the rotten fruit of their false world views.

Johnson, Philip E. *Darwin on Trial.* Downers Grove: InterVarsity, 1991. A University of California-Berkeley law professor finds the logic and evidence of Darwinism lacking. A fine critique of naturalistic evolutionary theory.

Lewis, C. S. *The Abolition of Man.* New York: Macmillan, 1947. A powerful critique of modern morality detached from moral absolutes.

———. *God in the Dock: Essays on Theology and Ethics.* Grand Rapids: Eerdmans, 1970. Many worthwhile chapters on various subjects.

———. *Mere Christianity.* New York: Macmillan, 1952. A justly famous defense of Christianity.

———. *Miracles: A Preliminary Study.* New York: Macmillan, 1947. A sharp critique of naturalism and defense of supernaturalism.

Lewis, Gordon, *Testing Christianity's Truth Claims.* Lanham, Md.: University Press of America, 1990. An excellent survey of modern apologetic methods with special attention given to E. J. Carnell.

Machen, J. Gresham. *Christianity and Liberalism.* Grand Rapids: Eerdmans, 1981. A classic defense of orthodox Christianity against theological liberalism.

Miethe, Terry L., ed. *Did Jesus Rise from the Dead? The Resurrection Debate.* San Francisco: Harper and Row, 1987. A debate between Gary Habermas and Anthony Flew along with respondents.

Moreland, J. P. *Christianity and the Nature of Science: A Philosophical Investigation.* Grand Rapids: Baker, 1989. Excellent analysis of the nature and limits of science and its relationship to Christian truth claims.

———. *Scaling the Secular City: A Defense of Christianity.* Grand Rapids: Baker, 1987. A significant and philosophically sophisticated defense of Christianity.

Moreland, J. P., and Kai Nielsen. *Does God Exist? The Great Debate.* Nashville: Nelson, 1990. A debate between a Christian (Moreland) and an atheist (Nielsen) with supporting essays by various Christians and atheists.

Morris, Thomas V. *Making Sense of It All: Pascal and the Meaning of Life.* Grand Rapids: Eerdmans, 1992. An approachable and interesting investigation with Pascal as the guide. One of the few evangelical books concerning the great French apologist.

———. *Our Idea of God: An Introduction to Philosophical Theology.* Downers Grove: InterVarsity, 1991. Involves the doctrine of God and is conversant with modern developments and written in an engaging manner.

Mouw, Richard. *Distorted Truth: What Every Christian Needs to Know about the Battle for the Mind.* San Francisco: Harper and Row, 1989. A winsome introduction to apologetics, especially helpful in developing the proper attitude and approach to defending Christianity.

Nash, Ronald. *Faith and Reason: Searching for a Rational Faith.* Grand Rapids: Zondervan, Academie Books, 1988. An able summary of the basic topics in philosophy of religion and apologetics.

———. *The Gospel God and the Greeks: Did the New Testament Borrow from Pagan Thought?* Richardson, Tex.: Probe, 1992. Challenges the syncretistic idea that Christianity borrowed heavily from Hellenistic thought.

Pascal, Blaise. *Pensées.* Edited by A. J. Krailsheimer. New York: Viking Penguin, 1985. Classic reflections on the meaning of faith and the defense of Christianity. *Pensées* is also available with a different ordering of the fragments with additional writings: *The Mind on Fire: An Anthology of the Writings of Blaise Pascal,* edited by J. M. Houston. Portland, Ore.: Multnomah, 1989. This also includes a fine introduction by Os Guinness.

Ramm, Bernard. *A Christian Appeal to Reason.* Waco: Word, 1977. A general introduction to apologetics.

———. *Offense to Reason: The Theology of Sin.* San Francisco: Harper and Row, 1985. A defense of the biblical doctrine of sin and its implications.

———. *Protestant Christian Evidences.* Chicago: Moody, 1953. An excellent treatment of the empirical evidence for Christianity.

———. *Varieties of Christian Apologetics.* Grand Rapids: Baker, 1979. A skillful survey of major Christian apologists through history such as Augustine, Pascal, Thomas, and Butler.

Schaeffer, Francis. *The God Who Is There: Speaking Historic Christianity into the Twentieth Century.* Downers Grove: InterVarsity, 1968. Probably the best of Schaeffer's apologetic books. Although his understanding of the history of philosophy was somewhat inaccurate, his apologetic method and sensitivity to culture was admirable and should be imitated.

Schaeffer, Francis, with Udo Middlemann. *Pollution and the Death of Man.* Wheaton: Crossway, 1992. Originally published in 1970. This edition includes a concluding chapter by Middlemann. Argues that the Christian world view, not pantheism or materialism, provides the best basis for sane ecology.

Sire, James W. *Discipleship of the Mind: Learning to Love God in the Ways We Think.* Downers Grove: InterVarsity, 1990. A follow-up to *The Universe Next Door* that further explores the implications of a Christian world view. Contains an extensive (but unannotated) bibliography.

————. *The Universe Next Door: A Basic World View Catalog.* Downers Grove: InterVarsity, 1988. A modern classic comparing the Christian world view with deism, naturalism, nihilism, existentialism, Eastern thought, and the New Age world view.

Trueblood, D. Elton. *Philosophy of Religion.* Grand Rapids: Baker, 1977. A systematic defense of Christianity as the most rational hypothesis.

————. *A Place to Stand.* San Francisco: Harper and Row, 1969. A concise apology for Christianity by one of its foremost modern defenders.

Yandell, Keith E. *Christianity and Philosophy.* Grand Rapids: Eerdmans, 1984. A rigorously argued study of key themes in the philosophy of religion.

Zacharias, Ravi. *A Shattered Visage: The Real Face of Atheism.* Grand Rapids: Baker, 1993. Although not a thorough philosophical refutation of atheism, very well written and points out weaknesses in atheism.

Ethics, Social Issues, and the Church

Beckwith, Francis J. *Politically Correct Death: Answering Arguments for Abortion Rights.* Grand Rapids: Baker, 1993. A philosophical and theological refutation of more than sixty pro-abortion arguments. A major work.

Beckwith, Francis J., and Norman L. Geisler. *Matters of Life and Death: Calm Answers to Tough Questions about Abortion and Euthanasia.* Grand Rapids: Baker, 1991. Covers the main issues on abortion and euthanasia in a question-answer format.

Bennett, William J. *The De-Valuing of America: The Fight for Our Culture and Our Children.* New York: Summit, 1992. A respected political leader offers important insights into the problems afflicting America, such as education and drug abuse.

Billingsley, K. L. *The Seductive Image: A Christian Critique of the World of Film.* Westchester: Crossway, 1989. A helpful look at a powerful cultural force.

Blumenfeld, Samuel L. *N.E.A.: Trojan Horse in American Education.* Boise: The Paradigm Company, 1984. A revealing expose of a powerful force in education.

Carson, D. A., and John D. Woodbridge, eds. *God and Culture: Essays in Honor of Carl F. H. Henry.* Grand Rapids: Eerdmans, 1993. Fine essays by established Christian scholars on areas such as law, medicine, philosophy, theology, and ethics.

Colson, Charles. *Against the Night: Living in the New Dark Ages.* Ann Arbor: Servant, 1989. A trenchant assessment of the decline of Western culture and a call for biblical faithfulness in the midst of it.

————. *The Body: Being Light in Darkness.* Dallas: Word, 1992. Important work on the nature and purpose of the church in the world.

Ellul, Jacques. *The Humiliation of the Word.* Grand Rapids: Eerdmans, 1985. An illuminating and compelling study of the eclipse of the written word by the image.

————. *The Subversion of Christianity.* Grand Rapids: Eerdmans, 1986. An important critique of modern Christianity by a noteworthy, if idiosyncratic (and sometimes unorthodox), social critic.

Erickson, Millard J. *The Evangelical Mind and Heart: Perspectives on Theological and Practical Issues.* Grand Rapids: Baker, 1993. Wise reflections on theological and social issues from a seasoned theologian.

Gaebelein, Frank E., and Bruce D. Lockerbie. *The Christian, the Arts, and the Truth: Regaining the Vision of Greatness.* Portland, Ore.: Multnomah, 1985. A collection of essays by a noteworthy Christian educator and musician.

Grant, George. *Grand Illusions: The Legacy of Planned Parenthood.* Brentwood, Tenn.: Wolgemuth and Hyatt, 1988. A well-documented expose of the origins and aims of this influential organization.

————. *Trial and Error: The American Civil Liberties Union and Its Impact on Your Family.* Brentwood, Tenn.: Wolgemuth and Hyatt, 1989. An indicting assessment of the most powerful legal force in America.

Groothuis, Rebecca Merrill. *Women Caught in the Conflict: The Culture War Between Traditionalism and Feminism.* Grand Rapids: Baker, 1994. Offers a new perspective on the debate between evangelical feminists and traditionalists by placing each belief into its historical and cultural context, and then evaluating each position in light of that context.

Guinness, Os. *The American Hour: A Time of Reckoning and the Once and Future Role of Faith.* New York: The Free Press, 1992. A magisterial analysis of the "American experiment" and the current "crisis of cultural authority."

————. *Dining with the Devil: The Megachurch Movement Flirts with Modernity.* Grand Rapids: Baker, 1993. A cogent critique of the church growth movement and a challenge to biblical fidelity.

————. *The Gravedigger File: Papers on the Subversion of the Modern Church.* Downers Grove: InterVarsity, 1983. Explores how modernity has affected evangelicalism with respect to pluralization, privatization, and secularization.

Guinness, Os, and John Seel, eds. *No God But God: Breaking with the Idols of Our Age.* Chicago: Moody, 1992. A powerful call to biblical truth in an age of compromise and subtle idolatry.

Horton, Michael Scott. *Made in America: The Shaping of Modern American Evangelicalism.* Grand Rapids: Baker, 1991. A jeremiad against evangelical accommodations to modern American culture.

Hunter, James Davison, and Os Guinness, eds. *Articles of Faith, Articles of Peace: The Religious Liberty Clauses and the American Public Philosophy*. Washington, D.C.: Brookings Institution, 1990. A fine collection of essays on the First Amendment and American public philosophy. Includes the Williamsburg Charter.

Kaiser, Walter C. *Toward Old Testament Ethics*. Grand Rapids: Zondervan, 1983. An important work by an established Old Testament scholar.

Kuyper, Abraham. *Lectures on Calvinism*. Grand Rapids: Eerdmans, 1975. Delivered at Princeton in 1898, these lectures systematically develop a comprehensive Christian world view.

————. *The Problem of Poverty*. Grand Rapids: Baker, 1991. A new translation by James W. Skillen of an address by the late Dutch theologian, journalist, and statesman.

Lovelace, Richard. *Dynamics of Spiritual Life: An Evangelical Theology of Renewal*. Downers Grove: InterVarsity, 1979. A historical and theological reflection on the possibilities for renewal in American culture.

Machen, J. Gresham. *Education, Christianity, and the State*. Jefferson, Md.: The Trinity Foundation, 1987. Penetrating and often prophetic essays by a Christian spokesman extraordinaire.

Mouw, Richard. *Uncommon Decency: Christian Civility in an Uncivil World*. Downers Grove: InterVarsity, 1992. A wise summons to convicted civility in an age of pluralism and relativism.

Mouw, Richard, and Sander Griffioen. *Pluralisms and Horizons: An Essay in Christian Public Philosophy*. Grand Rapids: Eerdmans, 1993. A scholarly study of the nature of modern pluralism and how Christians ought to respond.

Muggeridge, Malcolm. *Christ and the Media*. Grand Rapids: Eerdmans, 1977. A series of insightful lectures given by the inimitable British journalist.

Myers, Kenneth. *All God's Children and Blue Suede Shoes: Christians and Popular Culture*. Westchester: Crossway, 1989. A critique of popular culture and what it means to the church.

Neuhaus, Richard John. *America Against Itself: Moral Vision and the Public Order*. Notre Dame, Ind.: University of Notre Dame Press, 1992. A partially autobiographical and always insightful inquiry into the American condition.

————. *The Naked Public Square: Religion and Democracy in America*. Grand Rapids: Eerdmans, 1984. A pivotal book on church-state relations and the role of religion in American life.

Olasky, Marvin. *Abortion Rites: A Social History of Abortion in America*. Westchester: Crossway, 1992. A ground-breaking and in-depth study on the ups and downs of the abortion debate in America with suggestions for informed pro-life activism in the 1990s.

————. *Prodigal Press: The Anti-Christian Bias of the American News Media*. Westchester: Crossway, 1988. An analysis of the press in America and a theology for Christian journalism.

Postman, Neil. *Amusing Ourselves to Death: Public Discourse in the Age of Show Business*. New York: Penguin, 1985. A profound study of the nature and deleterious effects of television on American culture. Similar to Ellul's *Humiliation of the Word*.

————. *Technopoly: The Surrender of Culture to Technology*. New York: Knopf, 1992. A readable and challenging look at the dominance of technology in modern culture.

Rushdoony, R. J. *Politics of Guilt and Pity*. Fairfax, Va.: Thoburn, 1978. A substantial evaluation of modern liberal politics from a conservative Christian perspective.

Schlossberg, Herbert. *Idols for Destruction: Christian Faith and Its Confrontation with American Society*. Nashville: Nelson, 1983. A comprehensive and incisive critique of modern culture.

Solzhenitsyn, Aleksandr. *Rebuilding Russia: Reflections and Tentative Proposals*. New York: Farrar, Straus and Giroux, 1991. Written by one qualified as no other to offer his perspectives, which are valuable for Americans as well.

Van Leeuwen, Mary Stewart. *Gender and Grace: Love, Work, and Parenting in a Changing World*. Downers Grove: InterVarsity, 1990. Important observations from a Christian social scientist.

Veith, Gene Edward, Jr. *State of the Arts: From Bezalel to Mapplethorpe*. Wheaton: Crossway, 1991. Gives a Christian perspective on graphic arts and evaluates the history of Western art.

Wells, David. *No Place for Truth, Or, Whatever Happened to Evangelical Theology*. Grand Rapids: Eerdmans, 1993. A major work on the decline of theology and the rise of anti-intellectualism in modern American evangelicalism.

Cults, Aberrations, and the New Age

Albrecht, Mark. *Reincarnation: A New Age Doctrine*. Downers Grove: InterVarsity, 1987. A fine treatment of an important subject.

Alnor, William M. *UFOs in the New Age: Extraterrestrial Messages and the Truth of Scripture*. Grand Rapids: Baker, 1992. The most thorough and careful assessment of the UFO-New Age connection in print.

Ankerberg, John and John Weldon. *Cult Watch: What You Need to Know about Spiritual Deception*. Eugene, Ore.: Harvest House, 1990. Examines Mormonism, the Jehovah's Witnesses, the Masonic Lodge, the New Age movement, astrology, the occult, and false teaching in the church.

Breese, David. *Know the Marks of Cults*. Wheaton: Victor, 1975. Simply explains the key aspects of cults and contrasts them with a biblical view.

Clark, David K., and Norman L. Geisler. *Apologetics in the New Age: A Christian Critique of Pantheism*. Grand Rapids: Baker, 1990. A theological and philosophical critique.

Enroth, Ronald. *The Lure of the Cults and New Religions: Why They Attract and What We Can Do*. Downers Grove: InterVarsity, 1987. An explanation of the nature of cultism in its different forms and how Christians can respond to them.

―――. *Evangelizing the Cults.* Ann Arbor: Servant. A collection of essays on sharing the gospel with those in Buddhism, Hinduism, the occult, Mormonism, the New Age, Unity, Scientology, The Unification Church, and Jehovah's Witnesses.

Geisler, Norman L., and J. Yutaka Amano. *The Reincarnation Sensation.* Wheaton: Tyndale House, 1986. A thorough theological and philosophical critique of reincarnation.

Groothuis, Douglas. *Confronting the New Age: How to Resist a Growing Movement.* Downers Grove: InterVarsity, 1988. Considers how to respond to the challenge of the New Age with respect to apologetics and social action.

―――. *Revealing the New Age Jesus: Challenges to Orthodox Views of Christ.* Downers Grove: InterVarsity, 1990. Criticizes the New Age view of Jesus and defends the biblical testimony about Christ. Written to reach New Agers.

―――. *Unmasking the New Age: Is There a New Religious Movement Trying to Transform Society?* Downers Grove: InterVarsity, 1986. Describes and assesses the New Age movement.

Hanegraff, Hank. *Christianity in Crisis.* Eugene, Ore.: Harvest House, 1993. A major expose of the errors of the faith movement. Well documented and important.

Kjos, Berit. *Under the Spell of Mother Earth.* Wheaton: Victor, 1991. An expose of neopagan environmentalism.

Korem, Dan. *Powers: Testing the Psychic and Supernatural.* Downers Grove: InterVarsity, 1988. A professional magician and Christian explains how much of what purports to be supernatural is fraudulent. Seems to go a bit too far, though, in debunking all demonic supernatural phenomena.

Mangalwadi, Vishal. *When the New Age Gets Old: Looking for a Great Spirituality.* Downers Grove: InterVarsity, 1992. Written from an East Indian Christian perspective, this book treats areas (e.g., vegetarianism and tantricism) not often addressed in Christian critiques.

Martin, Walter. *The Kingdom of the Cults.* 2d ed. Minneapolis: Bethany Fellowship, 1985. A classic and encyclopedic treatment of the major cults by the father of the modern countercult movement.

McConnell, D. R. *A Different Gospel: A Historical and Biblical Analysis of the Modern Faith Movement.* Peabody, Mass.: Hendrickson, 1988. An excellent critique of the faith/prosperity teachings written by a charismatic.

Miller, Elliot. *A Crash Course on the New Age Movement: Describing and Evaluating a Growing Social Force.* Grand Rapids: Baker, 1989. A thoughtful and critical overview.

Molnar, Thomas. *The Pagan Temptation.* Grand Rapids: Eerdmans, 1987. A historically and theologically rich analysis of the modern drift back to paganism written by a traditional Roman Catholic philosopher.

Montgomery, John Warwick. *Principalities and Powers: A New Look at the Occult.* Minneapolis: Bethany Fellowship, 1973. A scholarly and fascinating look at the occult. Contains interesting historical material not found in most Christian books on the subject.

Morey, Robert A. *Death and Afterlife.* Minneapolis: Bethany House, 1984. An exposition of the biblical view of the afterlife and an analysis of its rivals such as universalism.

North, Gary. *Unholy Spirits: Occultism and New Age Humanism.* Ft. Worth, Tex.: Dominion, 1986. A large, in-depth, but sometimes idiosyncratic treatment.

Passantino, Bob, and Gretchen Passantino. *Witch Hunt.* Nashville: Nelson, 1990. Concerns false accusations made by Christians against Christians and how to avoid making them.

Pement, Eric, and Keith Tolbert. *The 1993 Directory of Cult Research.* Chicago: Cornerstone, 1993. This unique resource lists 729 agencies and individuals involved in a vast diversity of cult research. A very helpful tool. Not available in stores, it can be purchased for $7 plus $1.50 shipping from Cornerstone Press, 939 West Wilson Avenue, Suite 202C, Chicago, IL 60640.

Reisser, Paul, Terri Reisser, and John Weldon. *New Age Medicine: A Christian Perspective on Holistic Health.* Downers Grove: InterVarsity, 1987. Insights on how to separate the wheat from the chaff in holistic health.

Rhodes, Ron. *The Counterfeit Christ of the New Age.* Grand Rapids: Baker, 1990. A good response to false teaching.

Sire, James W. *Scripture Twisting: Twenty Ways Cults Misread the Bible.* Downers Grove: InterVarsity, 1980. An excellent study of how groups misuse the Bible. Also teaches us sound principles of biblical interpretation.

Spiritual Warfare, Satan, and Demons

Arnold, Clinton E. *Powers of Darkness: Principalities and Powers in Paul's Letters.* Downers Grove: InterVarsity, 1992. A study of Paul's understanding of principalities and powers with application to today's situation.

Anderson, Neil T. *The Bondage Breaker.* Eugene, Ore.: Harvest House, 1990. Excellent source for identifying and overcoming demonic oppression. Non-sensational.

Bubeck, Mark. *Overcoming the Adversary.* Chicago: Moody, 1984. Explains the ways of the demonic and how to approach it. Excellent sample prayers for deliverance.

Green, Michael. *I Believe in Satan's Downfall.* Grand Rapids: Eerdmans, 1981. Develops a biblical view of Satan and the demonic.

Kinnaman, Gary. *Overcoming the Dominion of Darkness: Personal Strategies for Spiritual Warfare.* Old Tappan, N.J.: Chosen, 1990. A sound study based on Ephesians 6:10–18.

Murphy, Ed. *The Handbook on Spiritual Warfare.* Nashville: Nelson, 1992. An important and comprehensive study.

White, Thomas B. *The Believer's Guide to Spiritual Warfare.* Ann Arbor: Servant, 1990. A clear directive on the fundaments of spiritual warfare written by a seasoned prayer warrior and counselor.

Christianity and Other Religions

Adler, Mortimer. *Truth in Religion: The Plurality of Religions and the Unity of Truth: An Essay on the Philosophy of Religion.* New York: Macmillan, 1990. Written to refute the syncretism of Joseph Campbell. Argues for a cognitive view of conflicting religious claims.

Anderson, J. N. D. *Christianity and World Religions: The Challenge of Pluralism.* Downers Grove: InterVarsity, 1984. A careful look at the exclusive claims of Christianity in relation to world religions.

Callaway, Tucker. *Zen Way, Jesus Way.* Rutland, Vt.: Charles E. Tuttle, 1976. A comparison written from a Christian perspective by a long-time resident of Japan and friend of D. T. Suzuki.

Clark, David K. *The Pantheism of Alan Watts.* Downers Grove: InterVarsity, 1978. A short critical evaluation of a leading exponent of Eastern mysticism in the West.

Corduan, Winfried. *Mysticism: An Evangelical Option?* Grand Rapids: Zondervan, 1991. A survey and assessment of philosophical work on mysticism along with a theological evaluation.

Fernando, Ajith. *The Christian Attitude to World Religions.* Wheaton: Tyndale House, 1987. An excellent introduction to the uniqueness of Christianity in a pluralistic world. Develops much of the material from an exposition of Paul's Mars Hill address.

Griffiths, Paul. *An Apology for Apologetics: A Study in the Logic of Interreligious Dialogue.* Maryknoll, N.Y.: Orbis, 1991. Argues that apologetics is an appropriate aspect of interreligious dialogue. Also discusses claims based on mystical experiences.

Groothuis, Douglas. *Myth and the Power of Joseph Campbell.* Powhatton, Va.: Berea Publications, 1990. A short monograph that theologically and philosophically critiques Campbell's syncretistic and essentially nondualist mystical views.

Hackett, Stuart. *Oriental Philosophy: A Westerner's Guide to Eastern Thought.* Madison: University of Wisconsin Press, 1979. A critical approach to eastern religions, including the prominent mystical dimension.

Johnson, David L. *A Reasoned Look at Asian Religions.* Minneapolis: Bethany House, 1985. An introductory and critical survey.

Jones, E. Stanley. *The Christ of the Indian Road.* New York: Grosset and Dunlap, 1925. Although Jones, a longtime missionary, was somewhat liberal theological he was a superb communicator of the gospel in Eastern settings. This book engages Hindus and Buddhists with the Christian message.

Mangalwadi, Vishal. *The World of Gurus: A Critical Look at the Philosophies of India's Influential Gurus and Mystics.* Rev. ed. Chicago: Cornerstone, 1992.

Written by an East Indian Christian. Looks at the major gurus of India, many of whom have influenced the West.

Netland, Harold A. *Dissonant Voices: Religious Pluralism and the Question of Truth.* Grand Rapids: Eerdmans, 1991. A careful and thoughtful study conversant with recent scholarship.

Otis, George T. *The Last of the Giants: Lifting the Veil on Islam and the End Times.* Tarrytown, N.Y.: Revell, 1991. A fascinating study of trends in world evangelization, the challenges of Islam and Hinduism, and spiritual warfare.

Richardson, Don. *Eternity in Their Hearts: The Untold Story of Christianity among Folk Religions of Ancient People.* Ventura, Calif.: Regal, 1981. An exploration of how much unreached folk religions can know of Christianity through general revelation.

Sanders, Oswald J. *How Lost Are the Heathen?* Chicago: Moody, 1972. A short but compelling account of the desperate need for world missions.

Wainwright, William. *Mysticism: A Study of Its Nature, Cognitive Value, and Moral Implications.* Madison: University of Wisconsin Press, 1981. A thorough and generally well-argued treatment. Consider especially the critique of Walter Stace's monism.

Zaehner, R. C. *Mysticism Sacred and Profane: An Inquiry into some Varieties of Praeternatural Experience.* New York: Oxford University Press, 1971. Important study on the reliability and typology of mystical experience. Written in part to refute Huxley's "perennial philosophy" viewpoint.

————. *Our Savage God: The Perverse Use of Eastern Thought.* London: Collins, 1974. Uses the Charles Manson killings as a focus for exploring the history and implications of the amorality monism and monistic mysticism.

————. *Zen, Drugs, and Mysticism.* New York: Pantheon, 1972. Written in response to the influence of Eastern mysticism on the counterculture.

Organizations That Count

Organizations dealing with the cults, the occult, and the New Age:

Christian Research Institute. P.O. Box 500, San Juan Capistrano, CA 92693-0500. Founded by the late Walter Martin, CRI publishes a quarterly journal, *The Christian Research Journal,* a newsletter, and makes available many tapes, books, and fact sheets.

Spiritual Counterfeits Project. Box 4308, Berkeley, CA 94704. Produces a journal, the *SCP Journal,* a newsletter, and provides tapes, and essays.

Organizations concerned with social justice and legal issues:

The American Center for Law and Justice. P.O. Box 64429, Virginia Beach, VA 23467. Another activist organization similar to the Rutherford Institute. Publishes a journal called *Law and Justice.*

The Christian Action Council. 101 West Broad Street, Suite 500, Falls Church, VA 22046-4200. A leading pro-life group concerned with legal reform and compassion for women with problem pregnancies.

The Christian Coalition. P.O. Box 1990, Chesapeake, VA 23327. A grass-roots political action organization that provides a congressional scorecard and other resources.

The Family Research Council. Suite 500, 700 Thirteenth Street, NW, Washington, DC 20005-3960. An informational and lobbying group headed by Gary Bauer that provides a monthly publication called *Washington Watch.*

The Rutherford Institute. P.O. Box 7482, Charlottesville, VA 22906-7482. A legal defense ministry, Rutherford is headed by lawyer and prolific author John Whitehead, whose vision is to preserve religious liberty for Christians and others against the encroachments of the secular state.

The Trinity Forum. 5210 Lyngate Court, Suite B, Burke, VA 22015. Led by Os Guinness, The Trinity Forum produces materials related to the Christian's public witness.

Audio Resources:

Mars Hill Tapes. P.O. Box 100, Powhatan, VA 23139-0100. Produced by Ken Myers, these sixty-minute tapes feature interviews with philosophers, cultural critics, and theologians on matters of cultural importance to Christians.

Notes

Chapter 1, "The Christian Mind"

1. John R. W. Stott, *Your Mind Matters: The Place of the Mind in the Christian Life* (Downers Grove: InterVarsity, 1973), 17.

2. James W. Sire, *The Universe Next Door: A Basic World View Catalogue* (Downers Grove: InterVarsity, 1976), 17.

3. Harry Blamires, *The Christian Mind: How Should a Christian Think?* (Ann Arbor: Servant, 1978), 43.

4. See Diane MacDonald and Dennis MacDonald, "Wisdom and the Apostle Paul," *The Reformed Journal* (January 1980): 12–21.

5. Sire, *Universe Next Door*, 24.

6. Chapter 2. See Romans 11:36.

7. Helmut Thielicke, *Nihilism: Its Origin and Nature—with a Christian Answer* (New York: Harper and Row, 1961), 142.

8. Herman Dooyeweerd, *In the Twilight of Western Thought: Studies in the Pretended Autonomy of Philosophical Thought* (Nutley, N.J.: Craig, 1975), 195.

9. Donald Bloesch, "Process Theology in Reformed Perspective," *The Reformed Journal* (October 1979): 21.

10. Westminster Confession of Faith.

Chapter 2, "Creeds, Slogans, and Full-Orbed Orthodoxy"

1. R. J. Rushdoony, *Foundations of Social Order: Studies in the Creeds and Councils of the Early Church* (Fairfax, Va.: Thoburn, 1978), 118.

2. John Warwick Montgomery, *Damned Through the Church* (Minneapolis: Bethany, 1973), 66–67.

Chapter 3, "The Meaning of Life: *No Joke*"

1. Erich Fromm, *To Have or to Be?* (New York: Harper and Row, 1976), 125.

2. Ibid.

Chapter 4, "Misology in the Pulpit"

1. Mortimer Adler, *To Speak and to Listen* (New York: Macmillan, 1983), 61.

2. Ibid.

3. F. F. Bruce, *The Defense of the Gospel in the New Testament* (Grand Rapids: Eerdmans, 1977), viii–ix.

Chapter 5, "Hebrew History in the Ancient World"

1. John Warwick Montgomery, *The Shape of the Past* (Minneapolis: Bethany Fellowship, 1975), 7.

2. I say theology and not philosophy because of Israel's theistic (and nonspeculative) viewpoint of history.

3. Harry Elmer Barnes, *A History of Historical Writing* (Norman, Okla.: University of Oklahoma Press, 1938), 22.

4. Ibid., 16.

5. Ibid., 16, 17.

6. Herbert Butterfield, *The Origins of History* (New York: Basic, 1981), 80.

7. Johann Gottfried von Herder, *Reflections on the Philosophy of the History of Mankind,* edited and abridged by Frank E. Manuel (Chicago and London: University of Chicago Press, 1968), 136.

8. Butterfield, *Origins of History,* 80, 81.

9. See R. J. Rushdoony, *The One and the Many* (Fairfax, Va.: Thoburn, 1970), 36–62.

10. Eric Voegelin, *Order and History* (Baton Rouge: Louisiana State University Press, 1958), 1:124.

11. Peter Berger, ed., *The Other Side of God: A Polarity in World Religions* (Garden City, N.Y.: Anchor Books, 1981), 30.

12. Ibid.

13. Mircea Eliade, *Cosmos and History: The Myth of the Eternal Return* (New York: Harper and Row, 1959), 104.

14. Ibid.

15. Berger, *The Other Side of God,* 34.

16. Gerhard F. Hasel, "The Polemical Nature of the Genesis Cosmology," *The Evangelical Quarterly* 46 (1974): 88, 89.

17. James Muilenburg, "The Biblical View of Time," *Harvard Theological Review* 54, no. 4 (October 1961): 231.

18. Ibid., 234.

19. Hasel, "Genesis Cosmology," 84, 85.

20. See Abraham Heschel, *God in Search of Man: A Philosophy of Judaism* (New York: Farrar, Straus and Giroux, 1955), 200–205.

21. Abraham Heschel, *The Sabbath* (New York: Farrar, Straus and Giroux, 1983), 7.

22. Ibid., 6, 7.

23. Hasel, "Genesis Cosmology," 87, See also William Dyrness, *Themes in Old Testament Theology* (Downers Grove: InterVarsity, 1979), 70, 71.

24. Butterfield, *Origins of History,* 37, 38.

25. C. F. Whitley, *The Genius of Ancient Israel* (Amsterdam: Philo, 1966), 70, and Robert C. Dentan, *The Knowledge of God in Ancient Israel* (New York: Seabury, 1968), 125ff.

26. James Orr, *The Problem of the Old Testament* (New York: Charles Scribners and Sons, 191), 36.

27. Dyrness, *Themes in Old Testament Theology,* 233, 234.

28. Butterfield, *Origins of History,* 81.

29. Ibid., 82.

30. Ibid., 84.

31. Ibid.

32. Ibid., 87.

33. See Meredith Kline. *Treaty of the Great King* (Grand Rapids: Eerdmans, 1963).

34. Christopher J. H. Wright, *An Eye for an Eye: The Place of Ethics Today* (Downers Grove: InterVarsity, 1984), 24.

35. Butterfield, *Origins of History,* 98.

36. Barnes, *History of Historical Writing,* 23.

37. Kline, *Treaty of the Great King,* 55.

38. Ibid.

39. Martin Noth, *The Laws of the Pentateuch and Other Essays,* translated by D. R. Ap-Thomas (Edinburgh: Oliver and Boyd, 1966), 87, quoted in Kline, 55.

40. Butterfield, *Origins of History,* 68, 69.

41. Ibid., 97, 98.

42. Ibid.

43. Ibid., 97.

44. Abraham Heschel, *The Prophets* (New York: The Jewish Publication Society of America, 1962), 169.

45. Ibid., 170. See also William McNeill, *The Rise of the West: A History of the Human Community* (Chicago: University of Chicago Press, 1963).

46. Butterfield, *Origins of History,* 97.

47. See Dyrness, *Themes in Old Testament Theology,* and Walter C. Kaiser, *Toward an Old Testament Theology* (Grand Rapids: Zondervan, 1978). For a critique of modern liberal biblical criticism relating to the Pentateuch see O. T. Allis, *The Five Books of Moses* (Nutley, N.J.: Presbyterian and Reformed, 1943).

Chapter 6, "Humility: *The Heart of Righteousness*"

1. Andrew Murray, *Humility: The Beauty of Holiness* (Old Tappan, N.J.: Revell, n.d.), 13.

2. Ibid., 11.

3. Blaise Pascal, *Pensées,* ed. A. J. Krailsheimer (New York: Viking Penguin, 1985), #148/171, 75. The first number is the Lafuma enumeration of the fragments; the second is the older Brunschvicg system.

4. Murray, *Humility,* 18–19.

5. Fénelon, *The Royal Way of the Cross* (Orleans, Mass.: Community of Jesus, 1980), 27.

6. Pascal, *Pensées,* #919/553, 316.

Chapter 9, "Information and Wisdom"

1. John Naisbitt, *Megatrends: Ten New Directions Transforming Our Lives* (New York: Warner, 1982), 18.

2. R. J. Rushdoony, *Bread Upon the Waters* (Fairfax, Va.: Thoburn, 1974), 67.

3. Richard Weaver, *Ideas Have Consequences* (Chicago: University of Chicago Press, 1965), 58.

4. Daniel J. Boorstin, "Homo Up-to-Datum Is a Dunce," *Reader's Digest,* September 1982, 54.

Chapter 10, "Putting Worship in the Worship Service"

1. Even when the worshiper is in a spiritual "wilderness" and does not feel the response of God, the work of worship is nonetheless a spiritually liberating activity and ought not be neglected for lack of immediate emotional reward.

2. Ben Patterson, *The Grand Essentials* (Waco: Word, 1987), 76–77.

3. This should not be understood to imply that God is dependent upon our loving him, as we are upon his loving us. God is utterly self-sufficient. He desires our worship; he does not need it.

4. C. S. Lewis, ed., *George MacDonald: An Anthology* (1947; New York: Macmillan, 1978), 2.

Chapter 13, "The Smorgasbord Mentality"

1. Ayn Rand, *Philosophy: Who Needs It?* (Indianapolis: Bobbs Merrill, 1982), 26.
2. Ibid.

Chapter 14, "The Quest for Revelation"

1. Carl Sagan, *The Dragons of Eden* (New York: Ballantine, 1977), 244.

Chapter 17, "Sports and American Character"

1. Blaise Pascal, *Pensées,* ed. A. J. Krailsheimer (New York: Viking Penguin, 1985), #414/171, 148.

Chapter 18, "The War after the War: *Reflections on the Gulf War*"

1. Blaise Pascal, *Pensées,* ed. A. J. Krailsheimer (New York: Viking Penguin, 1985), 56.
2. Ibid.
3. Adapted from "A Moral Code for Conflict," *U.S. News and World Report,* 4 February 1991, 52–53.
4. G. K. Chesterton, *The Common Man* (New York: Sheed and Ward, 1950), 52.

Chapter 19, "Ancient Assistance Against the New Age"

1. G. K. Chesterton, *The Thing: Why I Am a Catholic* (New York: Dodd, Mead, 1930), 174.
2. Patrick Henry, *New Directions in New Testament Study* (Philadelphia: Westminster, 1979), 282.
3. Joseph Campbell, *The Power of Myth* (New York: Doubleday, 1988), 56.

Chapter 21, "The Shamanized Jesus"

1. John White, "Jesus and the Idea of a New Age," *The Quest,* summer 1989, 14.
2. David Spangler, *Reflections on the Christ* (Glasgow, Scotland: Findhorn Foundation, 1977), 103.
3. Joseph Campbell, *The Power of Myth* (New York: Doubleday, 1988), 57.
4. Janet Bock, *The Jesus Mystery* (Los Angeles: Aura, 1984), 112.
5. Mark Prophet and Elizabeth Clare Prophet, *Science of the Spoken Word* (Livingston, Mont.: Summit University Press, 1984), 86–87.
6. Campbell, *The Power of Myth,* 56.
7. Cited in Otto Friedrich, "New Age Harmonies," *Time,* 7 December 1987, 66.
8. Shirley MacLaine, *Going Within* (New York: Bantam, 1989), 181.
9. Thomas Glanville, *Sadducimus Tiumphatus* (reprint; Gansville, Fla.: Scholars Fascimiles and Reprints, 1966), 10; quoted in Colin Brown, *Miracles and the Critical Mind* (Grand Rapids: Eerdmans, 1985), 41.
10. Blaise Pascal, *Pensées,* ed. A. J. Krailsheimer (New York: Viking Penguin, 1985), #352/526, 133.
11. For more information on the New Age view of Jesus see Douglas Groothuis, *Revealing the New Age Jesus* (Downers Grove: InterVarsity, 1990) and the booklet *The New Age Jesus* (Down-

ers Grove: InterVarsity, 1992). See also Ron Rhodes, *The Counterfeit Christ of the New Age Movement* (Grand Rapids: Baker, 1991).

Chapter 22, "Myth and the Power of Joseph Campbell"

1. C. S. Lewis, *God in the Dock* (Grand Rapids: Eerdmans, 1970), 66–67.

2. G. K. Chesterton, "The Unfinished Temple," in *G. K. Chesterton: Collected Works,* 28 vols. (San Francisco: Ignatius, 1987), 4:61; quoted in Gary DeMar and Peter Leithart, *The Reduction of Christianity: Dave Hunt's Theology of Cultural Surrender* (Ft. Worth: Dominion, 1988), 122–23.

Chapter 23, "Al Gore in the Balance"

1. Albert Gore, *Earth in the Balance: Ecology and the Human Spirit* (Boston: Houghton Mifflin, 1992).

2. Richard John Neuhaus, *The Naked Public Square: Religion and Democracy in America* (Grand Rapids: Eerdmans, 1984), 49–50.

3. See Walter Shapiro, "Gore: A Hard-Won Sense of Ease," *Time,* 20 July 1992, 29.

4. Cited in Ronald Bailey, "Captain Planet for Veep," *National Review,* 14 September 1992, 45. On global warming, see E. Calvin Beisner, *Prospects for Growth: A Biblical View of Population, Resources, and the Future* (Westchester: Crossway, 1990), 140–43; Edward C. Krug, "Save the Planet, Sacrifice the People: The Environmental Party's Bid for Power," *Imprimus* (July 1991): 4; and S. Fred Singer, "Benefits of Global Warming," *Society,* March-April 1992, 33–40.

5. Cited in George Will, "Gore Litters Political Landscape with New Book," *Eugene Register-Guard,* 3 September 1992, 9A.

6. Bailey, "Captain Planet," 46.

7. For a penetrating critique of Darwinian evolutionary theory see Philip E. Johnson, *Darwin on Trial* (Downers Grove: InterVarsity, 1991).

8. For an excellent theological defense of creation ex nihilo see Millard Erickson, *Christian Theology* (Grand Rapids: Baker, 1983–85), 367–69.

9. For a critique of deep ecology see Brooks Alexander, "Deep Ecology," *SCP Journal* 16:1 (1991): 10–17, and Stephan Elkins, "The Politics of Mystical Ecology" *Telos* 82, (winter 1989–90): 52–70. Elkins principally deals with New Ager Fritjof Capra's book *The Turning Point: Science, Society, and the Rising Culture* (New York: Simon and Schuster, 1982), which is listed in Gore's bibliography.

10. For a fuller treatment of this subject see Ian Harris, "How Environmentalist is Buddhism?" *Religion* 21 (1991): 101–14.

11. See the review article by Mary Lefkowitz, "The Twilight of the Goddess," *The New Republic,* 3 August 1992, 29–33, and Douglas Groothuis, *Unmasking the New Age: Is There a New Religious Movement Trying to Transform Society?* (Downers Grove: InterVarsity, 1986), 134–37.

12. For a Christian critique of the relationship of goddess religion and ecology see Berit Kjos, *Under the Spell of Mother Earth* (Wheaton: Victor, 1991), especially 75–109.

13. See Bailey, "Captain Planet," 43.

Index